which?
essential g

PR   RTY
INVESTOR'S
HANDBOOK

" This aim of this book is to help you to understand the many different ways to invest in property, including the pros and cons, what to watch out for and what to think about when working out what is the best way to invest for your circumstances. **"**

Kate Faulkner

About the author

Kate Faulkner has written extensively on property and is the author of three other *Which? Essential Guides - Buy, Sell and Move House, Renting and Letting* and *Develop your Property*. As well as writing on the subject, Kate has bought and sold property, renovated property for profit, invested in property for the long term and worked in the property industry for over ten years. Her website, www.designsonproperty.co.uk, provides independent answers to people's property questions in the UK and abroad.

essential guides

PROPERTY INVESTOR'S HANDBOOK

KATE FAULKNER

Very little would be possible without all the help and support I receive from Doug, my husband, and this book is no exception. While I work long hours, food and the household chores all get done around me and never with complaint. When I'm stuck, he listens and suggests how to carry on. Without him, my family and I would have a much tougher time, rather than a very enjoyable one!

Which? Books are commissioned and published by Which? Ltd,
2 Marylebone Road, London NW1 4DF
Email: books@which.co.uk

Distributed by Littlehampton Book Services Ltd, Faraday Close, Durrington, Worthing,
West Sussex BN13 3RB

British Library Cataloguing in Publication Data
A catalogue record for this book is available from the British Library

1 3 5 7 9 10 8 6 4 2

Although the author and publishers endeavour to make sure the information in this book is accurate and up-to-date, it is only a general guide. Before taking action on financial or legal matters you should consult a qualified professional adviser, who can consider your individual circumstances. The author and publishers can not accordingly accept liability for any loss or damage suffered as a consequence of relying on the information contained in this guide.

Author's acknowledgements
The author would like to thank Mark from RBS Associates, Steve from Hobsons, Stuart and Martin from Assetz, Tim from Property Secrets, Steve at Wolsey, Matthew from Global Property Guide, Tom from LandlordZONE, Paul from Belvoir, Denise from Moneycorp, Sharon and Simon from Conti Financial Services, Barry from CommercialPlus, Charles at Abbey National plc, Fiona and Emma at Property Frontiers, Charlton, Forestry Commission, Stuart at Humberts, Frank and Katie at Exchange Bond, John and Michaella from Paragon Mortgages, Maria at Easier2Move, Vanessa at Inspector Home, Leanne, Derek and Gavin from St James's Place, Richard at Trade Direct Insurance, Peter from Wilkins Kennedy.

Project manager: Claudia Dyer
Edited by: Emma Callery
Designed by: Bob Vickers
Index by: Lynda Swindells
Cover photographs by: Alamy
Printed and bound by VivaPress, Barcelona, Spain

Arctic Volume White is an elemental chlorine-free paper produced at Arctic Paper Hafrestroms AB in Åsensbruk, Sweden, using timber from sustainably managed forests. The mill is ISO14001 and EMAS certified, and has PEFC and FSC certified Chain of Custody.

For a full list of Which? Books, please call 01903 828557, access our website at www.which.co.uk, or write to Littlehampton Book Services. For other enquiries call 0800 252 100.

Contents

Introduction

Many people choose to invest in property because, whether you choose to invest in bricks and mortar or stocks and shares, it can offer good returns. But it is not free of risk.

There are four main ways of investing your money: cash, bonds, equities and property. Each of these is referred to as an 'asset' and each has a different level of 'risk' associated with it.

- **Investing in cash** as an asset is taking the money you have in your pocket and putting it in a bank or building society account that offers a return by way of interest.
- **Bonds** are loans to a company (or the government) that pay a fixed rate of interest with your investment repaid at the end of the term (a time period usually agreed upfront).
- **Equities** are shares in companies that can be bought individually or across a group and you may get back more or less money than you initially invested.
- **Property** has grown as an investment asset since the 1990s. Buy-to-let mortgages became available in 1995, giving people the opportunity to invest directly in bricks and mortar, and property prices have increased rapidly. As a result, investing in property has become big business. People are already relying, or hoping to rely, on property for additional or even full-time income. For some people, this may be the best form of investment, as it can be easier to understand than other

forms, such as stocks and shares. For others, it is considered an alternative to paying into a pension fund.

Deciding to invest in property to help secure a financial future is one thing, but doing it and achieving the returns you want or need is something completely different. For example, how do you decide where to invest? What types of property investment are available? Which one would best suit your circumstances? What happens if things go wrong?

The decision making is even more difficult due to the wealth of available information. Even worse, is the fact that much of the information can make property investment appear a 'bit too easy' or can be conflicting. In fact, realising a profit requires a lot of hard work and can often only be achieved via high-risk strategies. It is essential, too, that you verify any information you read with an independent adviser before you go ahead.

There are, however, enormous advantages to investing in property even though it isn't as easy as it might first appear. The key reason why property can deliver stunning returns is due to 'gearing', so it is essential that you understand this concept if you are to be successful.

UNDERSTANDING GEARING

With most financial investments, the amount you have available in your bank account is the amount that gets invested. So, £20,000 in your bank account equals £20,000 invested.

With pensions, the amount invested by you receives tax relief from the Government, so as a basic-rate taxpayer your £20,000 receives an additional investment from the government equal to 20 per cent (basic rate tax). Your £20,000 becomes £25,000 to invest. As a higher-rate taxpayer you receive 40 per cent tax relief via an adjustment in your tax code or, if self-employed, via your accounts, so eventually £33,333 can be invested.

You'd hope to get some kind of return on your financial investments – more than you'd get in a bank account. Over ten years, for example, you could double your money if a really great return was achieved, say on a product invested in the stock market, so you could draw out £40,000 or more at the end of your investment period.

With property you can 'gear' your investment; in other words, borrow against the cash you have to buy a bigger investment and reap greater rewards. For example, you could buy a property for £100,000 with a 15 per cent deposit of £15,000, have an £85,000 mortgage. Then use the remaining £5,000 from the £20,000 'pot' for costs, such as legal work, survey, gas and electrics. If the property doubled in value over ten years, it would be worth £200,000. Assuming you broke even on

renting it out, you would earn £200,000 minus the £85,000 mortgage and your £20,000 original investment. This means you would earn £95,000 on an investment of just £20,000. This is why property investment has delivered such great returns in the past.

This return does, however, rely on two very large assumptions:

- That property prices will always go up.
- That you can afford to pay the mortgage repayments every month, with a tenant's help towards the bill.

Without these two things happening, you can really end up in a terrible financial mess.

When gearing doesn't work

Imagine that you buy the same property for £100,000 and only let it for 90 per cent of the time. That would mean having to pay out costs of around £1,200 per year to cover the months when you are not receiving any rental income, but still have mortgage fees and other costs to pay. Over ten years you would have to pay out £1,200 per year while the property was empty – an additional investment of £12,000. Some maintenance was also required, which adds a further £10,000 to the property investment costs. So now you have invested:

- £15,000 in a deposit
- £5,000 in buying/selling costs
- £12,000 to cover costs when there is no tenant (voids)
- £10,000 in maintenance costs.

Furthermore, imagine that when you want to sell the property it has only risen in value by 25 per cent. The property would then be worth £125,000, so now the finances would be the property value of £125,000 minus £85,000 mortgage, £20,000 original investment, £12,000 of voids and £10,000 maintenance costs, coming to a total of £127,000. This means that instead of making a profit, you have lost £2,000.

Although these figures have been deliberately chosen to demonstrate that property can lose you money, there are many people that have genuinely lost money on property investments. Most prolific property investors would agree that they have had at least one bad experience during their property career.

SUCCESSFUL INVESTMENT

The key to successful property investment, therefore, is to understand what it is you want from it and how much time you have to spend on investing in property, from finding somewhere to buy, making any changes and, finally, selling on.

- Define your objectives from the outset, mapping the timescales of when you want to sell your investment.
- Surround yourself with a team of independent experts.
- Look at the different ways you could invest in property.
- Do plenty of independent research, continually checking figures and making sure that the investment(s) you choose really will deliver a good return.
- If you are already investing in property, as with any financial strategy, consider diversifying your investments.

Investing in property can be high risk, so understand how you can invest and the likely returns as well as who you can turn to for independent advice – and do this before you spend any money.

Main forms of property investment

In this book, the following areas are covered:

Buying off-plan: Purchasing new properties prior to them being built and finished.

Buying overseas: Investing in property outside the United Kingdom.

Buy to let: Purchasing a property to rent out.

Commercial investments: Buying, renovating and renting a commercial unit, such as a shop or office.

Land investments: Buying land, or areas that are predominantly land, such as a farm.

Property funds: A pool of money collected from investors and invested in property by an expert.

Property investment clubs (PICs): A club, sometimes called a company, that you can join to learn about property investments and/or make deals.

Property and pensions: Investing in property to deliver a pension in the future.

Property syndicates: A group of individuals who pool together an agreed sum of money to invest in either residential or commercial property. They are usually tied together by a legal agreement and can be managed or run by the individuals themselves.

Investing wisely

To be successful at property investment, the last thing you should do is rush out and find a property you want to buy and try to make money from it. Instead, approach property investment in exactly the same way as a financial adviser would with money to invest: do your research first.

1

Risk management

The first thing a financial adviser will ask you is what do you want from your money and when do you want it? Writing out your investment objectives is a great first step.

Typically, those people who invest in property do so for one or more of the following reasons:

- To gain additional income on a **monthly basis** from investments such as buy to let.
- To gain additional income on a **lump-sum basis,** such as investing money in a property fund, which will then deliver a lump-sum return, say, in five years' time.
- To become a **full-time property developer** and earn an income on an annual basis.
- To **retire early.**
- To gain **lump-sum money for a specific reason,** such as to buy yourself a dream car or to fund further education for the children.
- To **buy property for their children to live in** when they grow up, or to be sold to fund another property.
- To **purchase a holiday home.**
- To **rely on property for an income in retirement.**

❝Whatever your investment objectives, it is essential that you can measure whether or not they are achievable. ❞

Whatever your objectives, it is essential that you can measure whether or not they are achievable. Then you can see if your choice of investment is the right one for you, or whether you need to diversify to achieve your goals.

YOUR ATTITUDE TO RISK

For the independent financial advice industry, a person's attitude to risk is part of the conduct of business rules that financial advisers use for financial planning. It is a useful benchmark as it indicates whether to recommend investments that give a steady and more assured return or highly volatile investments that may – or may not – give a high return to the investor. Normally, the higher the risk you take, the higher the return can be. But don't forget that there is a reason for the following well-known phrase on all financial advertisements: 'The value of your investment can go down as well as up and you may get back less than you invested.'

An inexperienced investor's view is that property is one of the safest risk-free investments that you can make. And with property investment advertisement headlines such as, 'Become a millionaire in 12 months' and 'Earn £30,000 with no risk', it's not surprising people think this way. However, experienced investors know the level of risk involved, as most have had a bad return at some stage from part of their property portfolio.

To assess your own attitude to risk, visit an IFA, alternatively, visit the Financial Services Authority (FSA) website (see below). The chart indicating risk levels (below) helps to put the risk of property as an investment into context versus other ways in which you could invest your money.

Jargon buster

Gilts Short name for 'gilt edged securities', which are fixed interest or linked securities issued by the Government giving a more assured return on your investment

Managed funds Investment funds that invest in a broad range of shares or, more usually, in a broad range of other investment funds

With-profits funds Low-risk investment funds invested via an insurance policy or pension scheme. Your return is in the form of annual reversionary bonuses and a terminal bonus

Risk level

Risk levels are an essential planning tool for financial advisers to gain an understanding of an individual's attitude to different investment risks. Typically, there are two measures, one low to high and another on a scale of one to ten. For example:

Investment	Low to high risk	Scale of 1–10
Cash or deposit account	Very low risk	1
Fixed interest securities, e.g. gilts	Low risk	3–4
Managed funds, e.g. property funds and those with profits	Medium risk	4–5
Property and specialist funds, e.g. single market investments	Medium–high risk	6–8
Direct equity, e.g. investing in one company	High risk	9–10

Information supplied courtesy of www.rbassociates.co.uk

To assess your finances and help identify your attitude to risk, go to www.moneymadeclear.fsa.gov.uk and www.financial-planning.uk.com. See also the *Which? Essential Guide Save and Invest*.

Property investment risk profiles

The risk levels applied below are indications (rather than statistically calculated facts) given by professionals who work across the property investment market. They give you an idea of the lower and higher levels of risk that different types of property investment can incur based on the categories of 'low to high risk' as outlined in the boxes below and opposite.

In general, commercial property investment is less risky than residential as the long-term income returns are more stable. Another rule of thumb is that the longer you hold onto the property, the more likely you are to get a return.

Primarily commercial investments

These investments contain a high percentage of property and the remaining investments are non-commercial property.

Property syndicates: medium risk
These are typically a medium risk because you share the risk with other people and they are normally sold via regulated professionals albeit not officially regulated by the FSA, so there is no comeback on the institution if the investment fails.

Property funds: low–medium risk
These are typically low–medium risk as the risk is shared among many investors, they are fully regulated by the FSA and are normally invested in projects that have a track record of good performance. However, high risk is involved if the investment is highly geared in speculative property projects.

Commercial investments

These investments are 100 per cent in commercial property.

Tenanted property: low risk
Purchasing vacant properties: medium risk
When investing in commercial properties that are already tenanted, the contract tends to be for several years, giving you a finite return, even with pre-agreed increases. If you invest in un-let property, then you have an increased risk of finding a tenant to generate a return.

Residential investments

Buy to let: low risk

The level of risk here is considered low because property prices have typically grown over time so buy to let has a good track record as an investment. However, it is only low if you have done all the required research and ensured your figures stack up financially.

Renovate for profit: low risk

This is considered low for the same reason as buy to let. However, if you don't undertake due diligence, it is a high risk as your costs can go up rapidly and prices can come down around you, increasing the level of risk.

Build for profit: high risk

This is a high-risk investment for high reward. It's considered higher risk than other property investments as there is typically a higher investment upfront. Also, more can go wrong outside of your control, such as planning permission issues, the market turning and difficulty with tradesmen and materials. The more experience you have in this category, the lower the risk becomes.

Land investment: low–high risk

The risk of investing in land depends on what you buy, how long you hold the investment for and if you are using it to reduce inheritance tax (when it would be 'low' risk). Alternatively, you could make substantial gains from buying land with no planning, which would be considered one of the highest property investment risks you can take.

Overseas investment: low–high risk

Investing overseas can include any of the above property investment types and therefore varies considerably. Other factors that increase the investment risk profile include investing in countries with little history of investment returns, such as emerging markets (as opposed to France or America), as well as the economic and political stability of the country and if there is a sustained positive attitude to inward foreign investment.

Information provided jointly by www.assetz.co.uk, www.landlordzone.co.uk, www.propertysecrets.co.uk and www.rbassociates.co.uk

How much risk can you afford to take?

If you have £10,000 or £100,000 to invest, would it matter if you lost any or even all of this money? And are you willing to leave the money invested in property until it gives you the return you need or want?

It might be that currently you have a lump sum of £30,000 'spare'. However, you need to consider how safe you are in your current job and whether you will need some money for something unexpected, such as illness, that prevents you or one of your family, from working. It could be that your car needs fixing or the boiler breaks down and suddenly you need to get your hands on thousands of pounds.

If this is the case, you might decide to invest £10,000 in a low-risk investment such as a deposit account or fixed-interest earning investment, which means it is unlikely to lose its value and may grow a little over time. However, if you need this money tomorrow, you can still access it. The next £10,000 you might decide you don't need for the next five years, and you might not touch the final £10,000 until you retire, so are happy to invest for many years.

How will you manage the risk?

It is no good putting your life savings in to a high-risk property venture if you end up losing sleep every night wondering whether it is going to work or not; or if you are fretting about what would happen to your investment if you became too ill to manage it. In such circumstances, consider investing in property projects that are low risk, even though the return will be smaller. High-risk ventures are great if they pay off, but should not be devastating if they don't.

❝ Whether you are investing £10,000 or ten times that, can you leave it until it gives a good return? Can you afford to lose some or all of it? ❞

 For more about managing the risk, see making back-up plans on pages 19–20.

Investment returns

With property you should typically be looking at a long-term investment of a minimum of five years and many professional property investors look at investing for 10–15 years. So with such a long-term investment you must be 100 per cent sure you don't need to access that money in the time you need to invest it to get a return.

If you invest too much, too early, you might find you have too much cash in your investment, sell under pressure and lose money. The table below gives an indication of the minimum time you would need to hold individual property investments to start seeing a return.

LIQUIDITY

A critical point to understand, and particularly if investing via an IFA or with other people, is how liquid the investment is. How quickly can you cash it in and how much of it is under your own control? For example, in certain property funds you may be able to sell your investment and get out what money you can within a matter of weeks. If, however, you had planned to renovate

"With a long-term investment you must be sure you won't need quick access to your money."

Minimum investment periods before seeing a return

Property investment type	Minimum time to invest before seeing a return
Property funds	3-7 years
Property syndicates	5-10 years
Buying off-plan	6 months-2 years
Renovating for profit	6 months-1 year
Buy to let	5-10 years
Building for profit	1-2 years
Land investment	5-10 years
Commercial investment	5-10 years
Overseas investment	Varies according to the type of investment

Property prices can go down as well as up over time and these are just guidelines. Investment returns with property projects rely on your ability to carry out a successful project.

a property and have changed your mind and put it up for sale, you can only get your money out when someone buys it and the sale is completed. It is likely to take a minimum of three months and may even take a year or more if you don't price it appropriately.

Typically, shares and funds are reasonably liquid, unless they have to be invested for a specified period (see page 36), whereas a single property would be classed as highly illiquid.

THE VALUE OF HISTORIC RETURNS

You will see many charts in property investment documents (and financial ones) showing how property has 'outperformed' the market. When looking at the data, which compares, for example, a bank account to a property fund, this statement appears a fair description.

However, hindsight is a wonderful thing, and all regulated investments use the phrase, 'Historic performance is not a guarantee of future performance'. In the UK, people who owned property prior to 2003 have typically done very well, with residential properties on average growing around 100 per cent from 1997 to 2003. However, although some people have continued to benefit from price rises, others who bought post-2003 paid too much and are now selling in an over-supplied market for at least 10 per cent below what they originally paid. If such investors are able to hold the property for up to ten years they may yet be able to break even or make a profit.

So one of the critical elements when investigating any property investment is to look at the historic returns over a long period, year-on-year and over the last three months. Then look at the experts' predictions and use your knowledge and research to consider what would happen to your investment in a worst-case scenario (for example, a 10 per cent market fall or no growth) and a best-case scenario.

In property, there are some short-term investments that you can make, which will deliver within a year. But to be more certain of results and ride out any market falls, it is best to expect to invest for a minimum of 5–15 years, depending on what area you are investing in.

❝ When investigating investing in property it is crucial that you look at the historic returns over a long period, year-on-year and over the last three months. ❞

Understanding the market

When you start thinking about investing in property, it is easy to think that you know what you are doing. After all, you are likely to have rented at some point, so understand tenants. You may even have bought and sold a few times, so understand that process too.

And whatever happens, unless you are a stockbroker, you are bound to understand property better than you would be able to grasp stocks and shares or ways to make money from, say, buying and selling wine or from other forms of investment, such as art.

However, it is critical to realise that although you have some experience, being an investor is completely different to being a tenant or a homeowner. What you may hanker after and think is essential is likely to be 'personalised' rather than based on solid property investment experience.

BEWARE LACK OF REGULATION

Many of the companies you come across when investing in property are not regulated. If you are buying into some property funds, these must be regulated, but if you are buying an off-plan property through an investment club, then they may well be able to sell you whatever they want at whatever prices they like, with no guarantee that their seemingly attractive investment deal stacks up. As a result, if something goes wrong, you have little recourse.

CHECKING YOUR PROPERTY CAN BE TIME CONSUMING

Secondly, although you don't need to visit a company for investment purposes, it is essential to spend time visiting the site that the property is going to be built on or the property itself. If this is abroad, then the cost and time you need to invest can quickly add up.

FLUCTUATING PROPERTY PRICES

Property values, both residential and commercial, are not easy to predict, so trying to understand when to sell at the top of the market and buy at the bottom is even more difficult than dealing in stocks and shares. The property market can also turn very rapidly, within a matter of weeks or months, and if purchasers suddenly decide not to buy, prices can quickly come down as vendors need to

❝ Many of the firms involved in property investment are not regulated. This includes investment clubs, who offer no guarantees. ❞

sell. Whether they recover depends on the supply of property and the demand for renting/buying for that type of property in the area you are interested in.

SPREADING THE RISK

What is important with any investment is not to put all your eggs in one basket. If you were buying shares, you would generally buy into shares of multiple companies within the FTSE 100 or FTSE 250, rather than investing all your money in just one company.

This is much more difficult in property, especially if you want to buy to let, renovate for profit or build for profit. However, it is possible if you invest in funds or syndicates or even look at working with friends or families (with the right legal agreements in place. In these cases, you can invest in lots of different properties and spread the risk across the different areas, or if you are in a syndicate, no one person will bear the brunt of a downturn.

For example, if you had £30,000 to invest, you could look at putting £5,000 in a property fund, £10,000 in a syndicate and £15,000 in a buy-to-let or renovate-for-profit investment. Once you build up your investment returns over time, you can increase your investment in the areas that you find deliver the best returns for you.

With any financial investment, it is imperative to go through your investment strategy with an IFA. When looking at property investments, you need to ensure that the adviser is experienced at dealing with property investors; ideally they should also be a property investor themselves (see pages 27-8).

❝ If you invest in funds or syndicates, it is possible to spread the risk by working with more than one property. ❞

Exit and back-up plans

When you are researching the different ways that you can invest in property, one of the most important things to work out is how and when you are likely to cash in your investment. For example, if you are investing for your retirement and that is ten years away, then it is obvious when you will need to sell off all or some of your property investments.

EXIT STRATEGIES

Exit strategies for property investments tend to be fairly straightforward, in that you sell either on the open market, such as through estate agents, or via other routes, such as auctions, specialist subscription websites, such as buy-to-let-selling websites or clubs, or plot and renovation subscription services. During your investment time, however, you may wish to cash in some of your investments if you believe that they are at their height or indeed not returning what you hoped for and you want to invest in something more lucrative.

Once you've reached the time when your property portfolio is finally due to pay out, you can either put everything up for sale, or look at staging the sale so that you get the benefit of potential continued growth.

Be aware of tax implications

The most important thing to consider when planning your exit is your tax strategy and it is essential to do this BEFORE you buy, as you are then more likely to minimise the tax bill, while maximising the profit from your investment. A good tax plan can save you a great deal of money over time.

BACK-UP PLANS

With any form of investment, apart from needing an exit plan before you invest, you also need a back-up plan, just in case. It is all too easy to get into trouble with your investments. You may fail to consider all potential changes in your circumstances, which then, in a worst-case scenario, mean that you need to cash in your investments too early and suffer financially as a result.

 For more information on tax implications, see pages 202–6. See also the *Which? Essential Guide Tax Handbook 2008/9.*

The kind of scenarios that you need to ensure you have planned for are:

- **Getting divorced.** How would you divide everything? What would happen if investments are in your and your partner's name?
- **What would happen if you became sick** or a member of your family became ill and you needed to take care of them?
- **If you lose your job,** could you still fund your investments without losing your own home, for example?
- **If you have to put more money** into one of your investments, can you afford to do so?
- **What if your investments are less than you put in?** When do you decide to pull out? Can you pull out? How long would it take?
- **What if you were to die?** What would happen to your family? Would they have to sell quickly and still potentially owe money?

There are various ways to alleviate these problems should they happen.

- You can get insurance for critical illness or income protection against the loss of your job (although not if you have a buy-to-let mortgage). While paying out for insurance increases the costs, this might be worth it in the long run.
- Keep a contingency fund, especially if you are investing in individual properties. This could be, for example, enough to cover a couple of months' costs and one refurbishment – just in case you get bad tenants.

One of the best ways to help ensure that you are 'cushioned' if you have to sell quickly is to buy at less than the property investment was worth in the first place. For example, if you buy a property to renovate or let out from a syndicate or fund seller who has had to sell his or her share/investment earlier than planned, then you can hopefully buy at a discount. This could be anything from 10 to 30 per cent.

If you have to sell quickly, then to recoup the money spent on buying/selling the property, you will need to sell at more than you bought it for. This is 4–5 per cent for properties under £250,000 and, with increased stamp duty, 8 per cent over £250,000. You will have to work harder to find these deals, but they are a great way of ensuring that you don't get into serious financial trouble if your investments stop paying back or, worse still, start costing you money.

THINK AHEAD

Before you take the first steps into property investment, it's important to make sure it is absolutely the right thing for you and your family. Many people see it as an easy way to make money, but most property investments are time consuming, tie up your money for many years and can be risky.

To be successful, you really need to make sure that it is the right thing for your circumstances. You should spend time researching what investment is best for you and find experts to help you succeed.

Property investment toolkit

Television, newspapers and magazines are awash with people enjoying what appears to be an incredibly lucrative, often part-time, 'hobby'. Of course there are people who have succeeded, but there are others who, having lost money, wish that they had been more careful.

Get your priorities right

You may come across a property that you would like to buy to renovate or let out, at one of the many property shows and seminars. Here, speculators will try to tempt you with innumerable business opportunities, but think carefully about these potential investments – it is very easy to get carried away.

COST CONTROL

Before you even start your search, you must know exactly how much money you have to invest. This must be money that you can spare, and possibly afford to lose, and it must be seen as being available for the long term.

You may need to do a great deal of research, which takes time and money, and the cost will depend on the type of investment you are planning. For example, to research buying off-plan your main expense will be the cost of petrol for travelling around and visiting different developments. If, however, you want to invest in a similar type of scheme abroad you could be paying out thousands of pounds for airfares and hotel bills.

Start by working out exactly how much cash you have now. Cash is anything in a bank account that you have instant access to or money that you can get your hands on in a week. In addition to your cash, how much other money do you have and how long would it take you to access that money? For example, to cash in investment bonds may take weeks or even months. At this stage you should also be seriously considering how long you can afford not to have access to these funds if they were tied up in a property investment.

More importantly, do you have additional money to spare for emergencies? Many property investments involve tying up capital for five years or more – and a lot can happen in five years. What would happen if you lost your job, got sick or needed to move house – could you cover yourself without having to pull out of your investment?

"Could you cope if you lost your job or needed to move house, or had some other emergency?"

 For a list of websites relating to property investment evaluation, see Useful addresses on pages 211–13.

Typical examples of funds needed for buying property

Research

Subscription websites	Up to £500 per year
Books/magazines	£25–£150
Travel expenses	Budget for a minimum of three visits per property

Property evaluation

Survey fees	£400–£1,000 per property
Legal fees	£350–£1,000 per property
Finance fees	£200–£1,500 per property

Property investment purchase costs

Finder's fee	2–4% of the property's value
Deposit	10% or more of the property's value
Preparation costs	Depends on the property
Stamp duty	0–4% of the property's value
Property funds/syndicates	Charges made for managing the investment

Ongoing costs	Vary by property investment (see relevant chapters)

TIME CONSIDERATIONS

Success – which means making a profit – will also depend on how much time you have available to research opportunities and then to look after your property investment. Some investments, such as renovating or building for profit, require many hours on a daily basis before you achieve profitability. Others, such as buy to let, take up time on a monthly or weekly basis, while property syndicates and funds may take more time in the first place to research and check but subsequently are typically managed by someone else.

The old adage, 'You make your money when you buy' is particularly true of property. If you want to renovate for profit it may take months to get the right property at the right price. You may have to view and evaluate hundreds and visit 50 or more locations before you find the right deal. Narrowing this list to between five and ten, and getting quotes from builders, plumbers and electricians may mean it is months before you can make an offer. This is tough to do if you are working full time and have a family that you are responsible for.

After months of looking at properties for a buy to let and purchasing one or more, you may be looking forward to a rest, but you must immediately start managing your investment. Some buy to lets can be easy to take care of while others may have a tenant who demands hours of your time every week. If the rent isn't paid and you need to evict them, you may need to take legal action. These cases may sound extreme, but you must be prepared for all eventualities and make sure you have the time and energy to deal with them.

> " Managing a buy to let can eat up many hours a week, depending on how demanding your tenants are. "

Researching and managing a property investment

Investment	Research (minimum length of time)	Ongoing management
Property funds	Several hours per week for 3 months	Minimal
Property syndicates	Several hours per week for 3 months	Meetings on a quarterly/ annual basis
Buying off-plan	3–6 months, viewing 15+ properties	Minimal until completion, approx 2–3 hours per week during developments
Renovating for profit	6 months+, viewing 50+ properties	1–2 days per week to full time
Buy to let	3–6 months, viewing 50+ properties	2–3 hours per week per property
Building for profit	6 months, viewing 20+ properties	2 days per week to full time
Land investment	3–6 months, viewing 15+ properties	1–2 days per week
Commercial investment	3–6 months, viewing 50+ properties	1–2 days per week
Overseas investment	3–6 months, viewing 15+ properties	Quarterly visits

These are examples only; every property investment is unique and you should always work out the likely research and ongoing management time for your own project and ensure you have the time available to invest.

KNOW YOUR MARKET

Do you want to make money in the property investment market? Of course you do! An important part of your property investment toolkit is therefore to make sure you have a first-class understanding of the market you are investing in, be it investigating different property syndicates, property funds or the local buy-to-let market.

The person who will be affected if the investment does not deliver a good return is you (and quite probably your family as well), so it is your responsibility to make sure that nothing is left to chance. Always get information about investments checked for their accuracy, however 'thorough' the information you have been given appears to be, and don't be forced into buying a 'great opportunity' just because a company restricts you to a tight deadline.

Information is the key to success, and although you may (and should) have a good, professional team of advisers to help (see pages 27–32), their time will cost money. You should, therefore, do a great deal of the research about all types of property investment yourself before parting with any cash.

- **The internet.** You can find a wealth of information, some of it free, some of it not and, more importantly, some of it worthless. Whenever you see anything on the internet, check what the source is – an independent one or trying to sell you a specific type of investment? If it sounds too good to be true – such as making money overnight or a short period of time – it probably is! There are websites that give you property prices, assess property values and publish reports and surveys.
- **Magazines and the property sections of the newspapers,** especially the Sunday supplements.
- **Trade associations,** such as the National Association of Estate Agents (NAEA), Royal Institution of Chartered Surveyors (RICS) and the National Landlords Association.
- **Property shows and seminars.**

> **‘‘Always get investment information checked for accuracy, no matter how thorough it looks. ’’**

PLAN YOUR INVESTMENT

Property investment is all about money – your money – and making sure it delivers the kind of returns you want. Check and double check that your figures are accurate and don't trust anyone else. You need to become a real pessimist. For example, what if your buying or selling costs go up by 10 or 20 per cent? What happens if you get 10 or 20 per cent less than expected when you sell? What if you can't sell when you want to? It's no good being optimistic – if things are better than expected, treat this as a bonus!

Key planning points

1 Make a list of the costs involved and note the impact that an increase of 10 or 20 per cent would have on your returns.

2 Identify and get to know the market for your investment. Understand what your potential tenants want. You may like plasma screens, but your market may want to bring their own; you may want to rip out character features, but they may not.

3 Whatever you plan on spending, check the return from a financial as well as speed of exit perspective.

4 Time is money – it's better to get lower returns than lose a lot more through voids or mortgage payments.

5 Always put money aside, either to keep your investment going or to pay for the unexpected. Setting aside enough to cover three months of expenses of holding the property, such as mortgage payments and insurance, should allow you to sell quickly if required.

6 Remember the golden rule – only spend money on what adds value to your property, which means considering your buyers'/tenants' needs, not your own.

Once you have thoroughly done your research and found 5–10 potential properties/land or funds/syndicates that you are interested in, you must draw up an investment plan, which includes a budget and cash flow forecast.

It's important to have the cash available to spend as required, while the rest of your money should be earning interest until it is needed. Some property, such as building for profit and buy to let, will need ongoing injections of cash, so you will need weekly/monthly forecasts of available income to ensure that the investment period is fully covered.

 See specific chapters for advice on researching properties/land or funds/syndicates, together with information on preparing budgets.

Help and advice

It's very easy to think that you don't need advice, particularly if you have already bought a property, but each property is a unique investment in terms of funding and tax implications. While a property may appear to be sound, your investment could turn out to be riddled with expensive problems that you have to put right at your own cost.

Buying for yourself and buying to invest involve completely different considerations. When you first start, surround yourself with experts rather than attempting to do everything yourself. Finding a good team of advisers should be your priority.

INDEPENDENT FINANCIAL ADVISER (IFA)

To find an IFA, talk to other investors or visit property investment shows. Also read the property pages in the main newspapers to discover which companies are quoted or recommended for advice. When you think you have found someone, ask him or her the questions outlined right. It's important that you get

&& Surround yourself with experts - it pays in the long run.))

Questions to ask a potential IFA

1   How many of your clients invest in property?

2   Do you specialise in one type of property investment, or all types?

3   What services do you provide specifically for property investors?

4   How many meetings, or other forms of contact, would be required?

5   How much would it cost me to utilise these different services?

6   How and with what regularity would the investments be reviewed?

7   What qualifications do you have? For example, mortgage, investment or pension advice?

8   Are you registered with the FSA (see page 29)?

 To find out more about property investment shows, go to www.propertyinvestor.co.uk or www.investinpropertyshow.com.

on well and that your IFA can offer you what you need. Make sure that he or she is clear with you on what advice can be given, what advice is regulated (and so therefore what the IFA is liable for), and what your adviser is giving an 'opinion' on, which he or she could do for unregulated products such as syndicates.

A good IFA will assess your current financial and personal position and then be able to help you make choices between different types of investment. He or she won't be able to analyse and recommend that 23 Acacia Avenue is a good buy-to-let opportunity or give you feedback on how your property portfolio is performing, but your IFA may be able to help you understand the likely rent required to pay a mortgage and the other financing costs. Your IFA can also give you other property investment options to compare. In this way you can have a range of options rather than relying on just one deal.

Most IFAs will

- **Go through a 'fact find'** to get a detailed summary of your current finances, your personal circumstances and responsibilities and your investment objectives.
- **Research all the regulated property related investments** that may achieve your financial objectives within your risk profile.
- **Present and recommend** anything you may have requested advice on, such as mortgages, property funds, syndicates or insurance.

- **Probably recommend other advisory services,** such as for legal matters or property tax.
- **Organise the finance for any property investment,** such as mortgage and insurance.
- **Complete the paperwork,** such as applications for any investments and mortgage and insurance products, once you have decided what products you would like to use.
- **Regularly review your products** and financial situation.

❝ A good IFA should be able to understand the likely costs and give you other options for comparison. ❞

The cost of an IFA

IFAs usually charge by an hourly rate, which may be as much as £150, or will work on a commission basis. This is earned from arranging finance, insurance or investments for you.

PROPERTY TAX EXPERT

Property tax experts have to understand much more about property investment than just the tax side. They should have a wealth of knowledge and understanding that they will be able to share with you, and you can learn from them, particularly as their job is to assess the profit that property investors make on a daily basis. A good property tax adviser will:

- Assess your current income and tax obligations.
- Get to understand what it is you want to gain from your property investment. For example, you might want a regular income, lump sum or both.
- Consider and suggest different ways you can invest in property to achieve your objectives.
- Explain the best way to buy and maintain the property investment and the likely costs of selling, ensuring that any tax bill you have to pay is minimal.
- Submit any accounts to Her Majesty's Revenue & Customs (HMRC) on time, if required.

It is essential that any person/company advising you on property investment deals is independent from what is being offered. For example, there are companies specialising in investments abroad that will introduce you to their own services. While this is legal and you can meet to consider their advice, you should get the information from them in writing. It is then essential that you do nothing more until your independent adviser gives you his or her view and feedback.

The cost of a property tax expert

Property tax experts charge anything from £120 to over £250 per hour for the more experienced specialists. It's worth asking for a quote in advance of the time and likely cost it would take to go through your property tax information. A specialist may be able to assess your property faster, so although you pay more per hour, you may save on the total cost if he or she can do it faster.

❝ Property tax experts can teach you a lot more than just tax. ❞

For more information on IFAs, go to the FSA website at www.fsa.gov.uk. On the website you will also find a list of all registered IFAs. See also www.unbiased.co.uk. To find a specialist tax expert, go to www.taxationweb.co.uk/directory/.

PROPERTY SURVEYOR

Whatever your planned property investment, you should always get a surveyor who is experienced in assessing property investment projects to check the condition of the property and its value. It is a false economy to skip this crucial stage as not only do you need to know that the property is worth what you thought it was, but it may also help you to negotiate a discount, which will maximise your profit when you sell.

Surveyors have to be fully qualified and members of the Royal Institution of Chartered Surveyors (RICS). The RICS has specialist surveyors who can:

- **Assess a property's condition** and check for defects, giving a guideline on costs to put them right.
- **Evaluate a property's rental potential.**
- **Help and advise on a property's potential** for renovation/conversion/ change of use, for example, from residential to commercial or from a house into two flats.
- **Recommend on party wall issues** (required with structural changes to flats, terraced or semi-detached properties).
- **Help with planning** and building regulation applications.
- **Assess all of the above** with regard to land investment.

To find a surveyor, ask current investors, tax accountants or IFAs for recommendations. Some surveyors run estate or lettings agencies for either residential or commercial investments. Also visit property shows, read property investment magazines and find surveyors who are taking the time to write about their profession as they are more likely to be up to date with their information. You can also contact RICS and choose a surveyor from the website (see below), or contact a local branch of RICS for local specialists in investment analysis.

> **❝Always have a survey done by someone experienced in property investment projects. ❞**

The cost of a surveyor

Surveyors can cost anything from £500 for a survey on an average property to around £1,000 for a listed or 200-year-old building. For a commercial analysis allow for around £3,000 to ensure you get all the information you need before making your investment.

 For more information about qualified chartered surveyors, go to the Royal Institution of Chartered Surveyors' website at www.ricsfirms.org.

LEGAL EXPERT

You will require some sort of legal assistance with any property purchase, sale or investment. If you don't use a solicitor who understands property law, you could end up in a mess that could cost you any profit you had hoped to make.

The legal ownership of property is a complex issue, both in the UK and abroad. In the UK, most properties are registered, but abroad you may well find properties that are owned by whole families, and all members of the family must agree to the sale. Even worse, a property may be 'sold' by people who don't even own it and/or the land in the first place.

A competent and independent legal professional should check the documents for the property/land from an investment point of view and anything that may prevent your investment being viable should be highlighted. For example, if you want to rent out a flat, are there any clauses in the **leasehold** agreement that may prevent an owner from subletting?

Jargon buster

Leasehold Ownership for a set period, most commonly applied to flats and other shared buildings

Whatever your property investment, there will be legal documents to complete. If you buy at an auction, ensure you check the legal position before you go to bid and that your conveyancer can complete the purchase within the required 28 days. If the property is abroad, make sure that the expert speaks English and can convey everything to you without any confusion.

You may need to employ different types of legal experts, especially if you are going to have a diverse property investment portfolio. These can include someone who is an expert in:

- **Buying and selling property,** including such specialisms as new-build or listed properties.
- **Renting and letting,** with a knowledge of tenancy law and a detailed understanding of eviction processes.
- **Party wall and boundary law issues** between neighbours.
- **Property syndicates and property investment funds.**
- **Trusts, off-shore investments and inheritance tax.**
- **Forming property companies.**

A property legal expert will:

- **Review the legal paperwork** from you or the seller's solicitor.

 For more information on the legal aspects of property investment, see the *Which? Essential Guides Buy, Sell and Move House* and *Renting and Letting.*

- Ask about what it is you are planning to do with your investment, such as let it out or convert it.
- Advise on anything you have to consider or that is raised from the paperwork.
- Give you information on the legal aspects of finance options, such as any mortgage clauses.
- Carry out the legal paperwork to ensure that the investment is legally yours.

MAINTENANCE SUPPORT

If you have a property that requires ongoing maintenance, you will need a further team of professionals. Emergency cover for the gas, plumbing and electrics is essential, as well as a builder for refurbishments and maybe a handyman or a gardener. You can book these through a letting agent – but may be charged for the privilege – or you can choose your own people and hopefully build a good rapport so they are willing to work for you at a moment's notice. Alternatively, there are some companies that specialise in property maintenance for landlords or developers.

To look for good tradesmen contact the relevant association (see below). Other points of contact that may have lists of local help include landlord associations (see Useful addresses) or your local parish magazines.

> **!** The message to anyone tempted to invest in property is to do your research thoroughly and get involved only with your eyes wide open. Don't sign up for anything unless you are completely happy about every aspect of the transaction and an independent adviser agrees. Take responsibility for everything but ask for professional help, particularly if you have any doubts at any time about anything. Life as a property investor can be rewarding, but never let your guard down, not even momentarily!

The cost of legal advice

Legal costs can vary dramatically, depending on the amount of work involved. Ideally, if you are buying/selling property, try to get a 'no sale, no fee' fixed-fee conveyancing deal so that costs are clear. Charges may vary from £400 for an average £150,000 property to over £1,000 for a larger property or commercial building or for buying abroad. Get a detailed quote before you employ anybody.

 Relevant websites for tradespeople are www.trustcorgi.com (plumbers, heating engineers) and www.paintingdecoratingassociation.co.uk (painters, decorators). See also Useful addresses on page 213.

Property funds and syndicates

Property syndicates and funds are rarely covered in the media. They can be a relatively hassle-free way to invest for those short of time and low on capital or if you haven't enough money to invest in property directly.

Property funds

Property funds are a way of buying into the property market as part of a collective group investing in several different properties. Alternatively, for a lower-risk investment, you can buy into property companies that own, rent or develop property, so spreading and diversifying the investment.

In the UK, property funds are typically invested in the commercial sector and the income is earned through purchasing, leasing and selling commercial property. Property funds can be listed by the stock exchange, and you should find out whether any funds you are interested in are regulated or 'authorised' or whether they are unregulated, and therefore not protected by the FSA. If you take an unregulated product, you have fewer comebacks against the financial company who sold it to you than you would with regulated ones.

" You can invest in a property fund with as little as £1,000, and with the risks spread between several projects. "

TYPES OF FUND

Each of the main types of property fund are described on pages 36–9. Whichever one(s) you choose to invest in, consider carefully the pros and cons. Funds are described as being open or close ended. An open-ended fund has the ability to create more units or shares in the fund to offer to investors, whereas a close-ended fund has a fixed number of units or shares.

The difference between the two is that the price of close-ended funds can shift in line with demand for the units or shares as well as the performance of the underlying investments.

HOW DO YOU FIND A FUND?

There are various ways of finding out about property funds:

- Lists of property funds on financial websites such as the FT, Trustnet and

The websites for the financial companies described above are:
http://funds.ft.com/funds/, www.trustnet.com/ and www.morningstar.co.uk/uk/.

The pros and cons of property funds

Pros	Cons
• The investment can be as little as a £1,000 or £50 a month.	• You can't always sell 'whenever you want'. Money invested typically needs to be left untouched for 5–7 years.
• Lower risk as the money can be spread over several different types of property investment.	• No 'hands-on' involvement as with investing in a property, which is the reason why some people like property investment over, say, stocks and shares.
• In some cases, your liability can be limited to the amount of money that you initially put in to the fund.	
• The costs of running the fund are normally fixed (by a percentage such as 5 per cent per year) and usually with no requirement to invest more money to maintain the investment.	• If you do need to sell your fund, the market may be limited.
	• Sometimes, if too many investors withdraw their funds, the fund can 'close' and prevent other investors from taking out their money for six months or more. So make sure you can invest for the long term.
• Investment requires little ongoing maintenance/work, unlike a buy to let or renovation project.	• In comparison to other types of asset funds, the charges can be high.
• The investment can be clearly measured and evaluated against your personal objectives and possible returns from other investments.	• Some funds result in double taxation.
• Can be more liquid than investing in bricks and mortar.	

Morningstar (see opposite below), which give you information about the performance of each fund.

• Your IFA, who will be key in helping you choose the most appropriate fund for you.

It can be a complex task to compare the performance of one fund against another and then to evaluate and measure those performances in terms of other potential financial investments. As a result, comparisons of regulated products are probably best left to the expertise of an IFA, who is experienced in this type of property investment.

❝ Comparing the performance of funds can be complex. It might be something that is best left to the expertise of an IFA. ❞

35

Different types of property funds

Whatever the asset you are investing in – for example, whether it is stocks and shares, corporate bonds or property – there are several different types of fund that you can utilise.

Unit-linked bonds

These are life insurance-based investment plans where you invest a lump sum of money in a specific type of investment (such as property) and invest for either income or capital growth. Property versions of these mean that the investment is linked to something property related, such as the performance of the house price index. The gains will be paid out on a specified date, such as five years after the initial investment.

Unit trusts

A unit trust is a collective investment that works in a similar way to a share 'club'. The money invested by the individuals is pooled and a fund manager is appointed to invest that money. The trust deed will set out clear objectives of the fund (for example, to deliver income or capital, invest in the UK or Europe) and the manager will then invest with the aim of achieving those objectives. The fund is open-ended, which means investors can join or leave at any time and units are created or deleted according to demand.

Open-ended investment companies (OEICs)

An OEIC is similar in operation to a unit trust. It is also open-ended, so the number of shares expands and contracts as investors buy or sell their holdings. The big difference between an OEIC and unit trust is that an OEIC may have a number of different 'sub-funds'. You could have some money invested in a property sub-fund and another amount of money in a stock and share sub-fund, all held within the same OEIC. The OEIC itself is traded as a company so you buy shares rather than units.

❝Before investing, decide how much you want to rely on the property market to make a profit. You might decide that it's not for you.❞

Investment trusts

These operate in a similar way to a unit trust in that they are collective investments but operated as company and, as such, there are a fixed number of shares available. The value of the shares owned is calculated based on supply and demand rather than directly related to the value of the underlying asset. The biggest difference between an investment trust and an OEIC and unit trust is that an investment trust can borrow money and therefore gear your investment (see page 7). This can increase your return, but also increases your investment risk (see pages 10-11).

Property unit trusts

With property unit trusts, the properties (normally commercial) are held in trust (see above) and there may also be other property related investments rather than just investing in the fabric of buildings. For example, buying shares in companies that invest in property projects as well as some that may invest and carry out the property project themselves. There are two main types of property unit trust: authorised and unauthorised.

AUTHORISED property unit trusts are regulated by the FSA and are mainly intended for the private investor. They are not geared (see page 7) so the money you invest is the maximum you could lose. Liquidity is typically good as you can usually buy or sell whenever you want to, either back to the fund or on the open market. You share the costs of investing in property with other investors and they are an easy way to diversify your portfolio.

However, because you can't gear your investment, you will only ever be able to grow your original investment, rather than make full use of all that you can borrow, as with other types of property investment.

UNAUTHORISED property unit trusts are not regulated by the FSA and so cannot be marketed to the general public. However, the people who are responsible for running these funds still have to be regulated by the FSA so it's not as scary as it might at first appear to be. These are not accessible to all investors, so you will need to consult with your IFA to see if you are eligible.

They are not very liquid because you only have the option of selling your investment to other people in the fund, so it may not be easy to convert them in to cash should the need arise.

Property investment companies (PICs)

PICs are basically the 'big property investors'; companies specifically set up to buy and invest in property, but unlike PUTs, they never sell their property investments. If you want to cash in your investment, you sell it back to the company and not on the open market.

The advantages of a PIC are that you can put money into a PIC and take it out at any time as long as the company has the funds to buy back your shares. The companies are regulated and use the collective power of their investors to take advantage of diverse property investments. They also have long-term strategies, which are both very specific and proactive, to increase the money that you invest. They are able to put your money into development projects rather than just investing in existing properties and their growth.

However, the high levels of liquidity in these funds mean that they can be volatile, reacting in a similar way to stocks and shares. As a result they are best viewed as a long-term investment. Research and management costs may also be higher than with other funds, so you may find that your original investment may go down in the first few years, until the fund begins to generate a return.

Real estate investment trusts (REITs)

A REIT is a UK company listed on the stock market that runs a rental business. You can invest in them by buying shares. REITs invest primarily in commercial property (some do invest in mixed property developments and thus indirectly in residential properties).

REITs have all the good points of other funds – including great liquidity, portfolio diversification and regulation by the FSA. They are also more tax-efficient than other property funds. All the profits are distributed directly to the investors so there is no company tax bill to be deducted from the investment's earnings (although this income is taxable once received by the investor).

On the other hand, they have high operational costs and the investments are mostly limited to the commercial market.

Before you invest

When considering investing in property funds, it is important to discuss your investment objectives with an IFA who specialises in these funds, and you should be able to find someone local to you on www.unbiased.co.uk.

However, here is a breakdown of information that is useful to know when considering different types of property fund investments.

- Most funds that invest in property invest in commercial as opposed to residential property.
- Whichever type of fund you invest in, your money is invested in one of the following ways:
  - Purely in property.
  - Around 80 per cent of your funds in property and the rest in shares, bonds and even cash.
  - Some companies have funds that buy and own property, others just buy shares in companies that invest in property and some do both.
- Before investing, decide (with a financial adviser) how much you want to rely on the property market for your investment returns or whether you want to spread the risk with other asset classes.
- Some of the funds are regulated by the FSA, but not all and again you need to decide whether this is an important requirement when investing your money.

For more information about property funds, go to:

The Association of Real Estate Funds: www.aput.co.uk/home.html

Directgov: www.direct.gov.uk/en/MoneyTaxAndBenefits/
   ManagingMoney/SavingsAndInvestments/DG_10034496

Reita: www.reita.org

WHAT RETURN CAN YOU EXPECT?

We are continually warned with **shares** that they will each return different profits. In addition, there are also high risks involved in investing in this way and the value of our funds may go down in real terms (by not keeping pace with inflation, or if property values fall) as well as going up in value.

As with all financial investments, the performance of any property fund relies on the expertise of the **fund manager**. Your fund will only reach its full potential, and hopefully grow in line with your objectives, if managed proficiently and in a professional way.

In the past, property fund marketing and performance claims have come in for some criticism by the **FSA** for not giving the full picture of the risk and potential return of property investment. There is, however, a trade association for these funds, which companies can choose to join, called the Association of Real Estate Funds (AREF). It represents the real estate fund sector while seeking to raise awareness of real estate funds. Membership is voluntary and some of its key aims are to 'promote excellence and transparency in performance measurement and provide funding for indices and related publications'.

Other companies that analyse and rate the financial strength and performance of funds include Standard and Poors, and Micropal, but these are mainly used by financial advisers.

> **" Property funds have been criticised for not giving the full picture, but their trade association AREF aims to promote transparency. "**

To find out more about AREF, go to www.aref.org.uk. The association produces a quarterly guide to property fund investment returns, which you can find by going to www.aref.org.uk/performance.html.

Property fund performance

These figures show that over a five-year period AREF members (excluding APUTs) property funds have delivered a 16% return – matching the FTSE all-share index. However, within these pooled figures, there are dramatic variations of fund performance with some gaining nearly 40% and others as low as 5%.

	All pooled property funds index	FTSE all-share index
Quarter	-1.7	-1.8
Year to date	2.7	5.7
1 year	6.9	12.2
3 year [1]	16.5	17.1
5 year [1]	15.9	16.8

[1] Denotes annualised figures and this information is based on data provided to the end of December 2007.

Ths information is derived from the IPD PPF Indices, sponsored by HSBC and AREF

ASSESSING FUNDS

Choosing which fund to invest in is fairly simple: it's the one that matches your investment objectives (see pages 22–6), such as to gain more income or to save for a lump sum at a future date. Other things that you need to consider are:

- How long can you invest for?
- Can you invest this money for the full term under ANY circumstances?

- Do you want to invest in a fund that merely invests the money that has been put in to it, or one that uses your money to 'gear up' (see page 7) in order to borrow more money to invest further? This last is a riskier proposition.

❝Choose the fund that matches your objectives, such as generating income or saving a lump sum.❞

For more information about investing, see the *Which? Essential Guide Save and Invest* and www.assetz.co.uk. See also www.ipf.org.

Property syndicates

If you are someone who is interested in property funds but would like a more hands-on investment, it is worth considering property syndicates. They work in a similar way to funds, but with a few differences.

The differences between property funds and property syndicates are:

- Investors own 100 per cent of the properties within the syndicate.
- There may be up to 15 members, all of whom have equal voting rights on decisions.
- Property managers are usually employed to look after the investments that are made.

- They are not regulated by the FSA, although the authority is looking into regulation.
- The investment required ranges from £20,000 to £50,000 or more.
- Syndicates can be created as a **limited company**, **partnership** or trust fund.

The main difference between syndicates and most other investments is that if you want to sell them, you will either have to persuade someone else in the syndicate to buy you out or find someone else outside the syndicate.

❝If you want to leave a syndicate, you have to find a buyer.❞

The pros and cons of syndicates

Pros	Cons
• You can invest smaller amounts of money than if buying alone.	• Fixed time limit of five years plus to invest low liquidity.
• You can gear your own money more by sharing the syndicate purchases with other members.	• Limited market to sell to, as long as you do so before the end of the investment period.
• You can limit your liability, which you couldn't do if buying a property on your own.	• You can't always have hands-on experience of the properties.
	• Difficult to source as some work on an invitation-only basis via an IFA.

Jargon buster

Limited company A business enterprise where the shareholders' liability for any losses or debts is restricted to the company as opposed to the directors

Partnership A company set up by two or more people who put money in to the business and share the financial risks and profits

FINDING A SYNDICATE AND GETTING A RETURN

Syndicates are normally organised and/or run by accountants, solicitors and IFAs.

It is traditionally difficult to find out the returns generated by syndicates since they are not regulated. Consequently, finding a syndicate involves looking for several that are in the process of being set up or alternativly where they are already being run and somebody in the syndicate wants to sell their share.

The priority is to find a syndicate that meets your investment objectives and where you are comfortable with the level of risk involved. You should also be happy about:

- The other members.
- How the syndicate is run.
- How the properties are managed.

Ideally find more than one syndicate and compare the costs involved. For example, do you have to pay a percentage of the investment just to become a member and, once involved, are there ongoing annual costs to run it? Should you decide to leave, would it also cost you money to do that? Unless you are able to find out what these costs are, you will be unable to discover your likely return.

“ The ideal method is to find more than one syndicate that matches your objectives so that you can compare the costs involved. ”

 To find out more about accessing syndicates, go to www.assetz.co.uk and www.attivo.com.

David and Rebecca are in their sixties. They are retiring and David has sold his marketing business. They have cleared their mortgage and have enough cash left over to reinvest for later in life. They are happy to take on some risk for the chance of a good return. David is used to arranging his own financial investments, so decides to research and choose the funds himself, even though he has no experience of the property market.

Scenario

- David invests £10,000 in a bond, which pays out £13,000 in five years' time, giving a gross gain of £3,000. Growth of 30 per cent, or 6 per cent per annum.
- He invests £10,000 in a property fund, which pays out £15,000 in ten years' time, giving a gross gain of £5,000. Growth of 50 per cent, or 5 per cent per annum.
- He invests £50,000 in a syndicate, which pays out £125,000 in 15 years' time, giving a gross gain of £75,000. Growth of 150 per cent or 10 per cent per annum.

None of these returns is spectacular, and it may have been better if David had sought advice from an IFA, but they are likely to have beaten returns received from a bank account or other less risky investments. However, the money was tied up for quite long periods and some couldn't be cashed in until specific dates. But at least they had little of their retirement time taken up with lots of effort on a buy to let or renovating property.

To check how well such funds grow in comparison to other investments, check with an IFA what would happen if the money was put into other assets, such as being invested in stocks and shares. Clerical Medical's 'Assetwatch' is a biannual study that tracks the value of five asset classes over time and is a valuable research tool. The asset classes are shares (UK and International), bonds (UK and International), cash, property (UK Commercial and Residential) and commodities (All Commodities and Precious Metals) and can be found at www.clericalmedical.co.uk.

Buying off-plan

Buying off-plan means buying a property before it has been built. It is a highly speculative form of investment and works well when a large, real discount is negotiated from the developer and property prices are increasing fast.

Planning for success

Early in 2000, when property prices were growing at 10 per cent year on year and sometimes 25 per cent or more on an annual basis, buying off-plan for investment became extremely popular in the UK.

As property prices continued to rise, it was possible to put down a 10 per cent deposit with a developer and then sell on to a new buyer either before or at completion. For example, a property worth £100,000 could be purchased with a £10,000 deposit and sold after a 20 per cent price rise for £120,000. In this way, the investor could make £20,000, less costs, for a short-term investment of only £10,000.

Unfortunately, this method of buying property off-plan, known as 'flipping' or a back-to-back transaction, is no longer the foolproof way to make money that it once was in the UK. Investors, having already paid prices that were too high, have, in some cases, even seen values fall due to over supply. Combined with a general slowdown in the market, opportunities are few and far between and the idea of making a quick and 'easy' profit is unlikely, unless the market starts to grow again.

When buying and selling a property off-plan, you will incur approximately 5 per cent buying and selling costs for properties under £250,000, and 8 per cent for properties over that figure. As a result, just to cover these costs and break even, you need to find a buyer willing to purchase at least 5 or 8 per cent above what you originally paid for the property. Many people who would previously have invested in this way are struggling to see these immediate returns in property price growth. Instead, they are securing off-plan properties at as big a discount as possible with the intention of holding them for the longer term as a buy-to-let investment.

You can still make money through buying off-plan, but only if you buy the right property in the right area at the right price and the location is experiencing high price growth. If you get it wrong, you could be selling at a substantial discount at an auction, potentially losing a great deal of money. Before going any further, look at the potential costs outlined opposite for buying a property off-plan.

 For more information about buy-to-let investments, see pages 84–90.

The pros and cons of buying off-plan

Pros

- Potentially good return on initial money invested as long as the market is rising.
- Potential low outlay as you only need to invest for the deposit and can now cover this money with an insurance product (if you sell at the same time as you complete on the property).
- Little work as you don't have to manage or renovate the property.

Cons

- Finding the right investment isn't especially easy.
- New builds are typically sold at a premium, so prices have to rise substantially – and at a fast rate to make a return.
- High risk as property prices can turn within months and what seemed like a good investment can easily lose you money.
- If you buy too early, by the time you come to sell the property, the demand in the area could have changed and you end up competing with better, cheaper properties.

Off-plan property costs to consider

Initial reservation

Reservation fees	Around £1,000
Deposit	5–10% of the property's value (or Exchange Bond – see box, page 50)
Legal fees	Vary from £300 to over £1,000

On completion

Balance of monies	90–95% of the property's value
Final legal fee	Around £150

Ongoing (for leasehold properties and some new-build developments)

Service charges	Varies by development
Ground rent	Varies by development
Buy-to-let fees	See pages 100–1
Stamp duty	If you sell after you have completed on the property

CRITICAL SUCCESS FACTORS

The three critical success factors in buying off-plan are research, negotiation and ensuring that you have a back-up plan if you want to 'flip' but can't.

Researching the opportunities

- **Approach a developer as early as possible.** Developers want to recoup the cost of the land and construction as quickly as possible. Sales and reservations already 'in the bag' at launch will both help their cash flow and give credibility to their project, so talk to them as early as possible as they will have an incentive to sell to you at a discount. If you can, approach the developer either before or as soon as the plans have been approved by the local council and be one of the first to see what is on offer. You can even see the site development from the plans submitted to the local authority.
- **Look at the site layout and assess which are the prime properties.** Those that will attract the most interest have unique features, for example, penthouse flats and those with balconies, and anything on the top floor, which has few or no neighbours. With houses you should look for decent-sized plots, anything at the end of a terrace or any other special features.

❝ For the best chance of success, research your opportunities and negotiate a good price. ❞

- **Visit the site and research the area.** Find out what local prices are like for anything with a similar specification to yours, both for new-build and in the second-hand market:
  - Are these prices likely to increase and at the same rate for both types of property?
  - Is the local population growing or declining, young or older?
  - Talk to local estate and lettings agents; is there a shortage or an over-supply of any particular type of property?
  - If you are buying to let, find out the local rental figures by talking to letting agents, reading the local property papers and visiting properties for rent so you can assess why some are worth more than others.

All these questions will help to identify potential future demand and whether this is the investment for you.

Remember to never solely rely on information from one developer, agent or property investment club as they have a vested interest in selling, and at the highest price. Get independent advice from a local surveyor.

Negotiating a good price

Getting the best deal you can depends on the developer's circumstances. Developers fall broadly in to three categories:

- Large national companies, such as Barratt and Redrow.
- Medium-sized (sometimes regional) ones, such as Banner Homes or Antler.
- Small local builders.

If it is year-end or they are desperate for a sale or reservation to launch or close the site, your negotiating position may be more favourable.

Discounts range from 5 to 25 per cent depending on a number of factors, including how many properties you intend to purchase. There may be a straight reduction in the price or incentives such as the developer offering to pay the stamp duty or upgrading the property specification.

The critical success factor here is making sure that the discount is real and that the developer isn't giving the discount off an already inflated price. With a new-build development you are paying for benefits such as structural guarantees and the very latest building regulation standards. If developers think that property prices may grow over the period they are selling, they may well also factor in this predicted price rise from the start. It could be as much as 10–20 per cent more than for similar properties on the second-hand market.

Your back-up plan

If prices fall, due either to market conditions or because there is an over-supply of properties on the site, it becomes a buyer's market and you may not want to sell. If this were to happen, you need to make sure that you could continue to cover all your costs. You may need to hold on to the property for a few years and use it as a buy to let, but just in case there is an over supply of properties to let, make sure you can afford to be the cheapest and cover

 Remember that developers will often give ordinary buyers incentives, such as including carpets and/or appliances, arranging a part-exchange deal or paying legal and other costs, such as stamp duty. You must make sure that your discount is better than the average one given or you aren't really getting a discount at all.

your costs as much as possible. It is better to do this than to make no profit or be forced to sell at a loss.

To manage the risks of buying off-plan you need to buy wisely and use all the information at your disposal. If you want to 'flip' the property, for example, make sure that there is going to be a demand for it and there are not 100 other investors in the same block with the same idea. Always have a back-up plan in place. For example, if all else fails, make sure you can afford to keep the property on as a buy to let until the markets recover. If buying specifically as a buy to let, make sure you have researched what other new-build completions (your development and its competitors) are going to be available at the same time as yours. Be careful not to buy into a development or area that is going to have a huge supply of new builds all at once.

Finance and legal checks

There are two elements to funding an off-plan property. First there is the initial payment to be made upfront and then there are the ongoing finances to consider.

UPFRONT COSTS

Reserving the property can cost up to £1,000, but this is usually refundable within 28 days if you need to pull out for any reason. You will then need to instruct your solicitor, who should be an independent legal adviser experienced in new-build contracts.

Make sure that the solicitor is acting solely on your behalf and is not someone who has been recommended by the developer, even if they offer to pay your fees.

The developer is likely to insist on an exchange within the 28-day period of reserving the property at which point the deposit has to be paid. This is normally 10 per cent for properties over £100,000 or 5 per cent for properties that are priced lower than that.

Alternatively, you can take out an Exchange Bond (see below).

Exchange Bonds

This is an insurance policy for developers, which allows you to retain your deposit monies until completion, but guarantees that you will then pay the balance in full. Not all developers accept this type of bond, but if they do you will be able to earn interest on your money while the legal process is being finalised. The cost of an Exchange Bond varies according to the amount of the deposit, but is typically around £725 for an Exchange Bond of £20,000 (house purchase price £200,000) to cover a six-month period between exchange and completion.

An Exchange Bond can be purchased via an IFA or through a house builder and there are two types to consider.

- The General Exchange Bond is used with existing housing stock, and allows you to pay the deposit on completion.
- The Term Exchange Bond is used with new homes off-plan and is an option that allows you to delay paying the deposit for a period of three months to four years. This can be useful if your deposit is coming from investments that need notice of a month or more, or if you want to pay the deposit only once your existing property has been sold.

If you default for any reason, the insurer will seek to recover the deposit monies owed. For more information, go to www.exchangebond.com.

Ten steps to financing an off-plan property

Ideally, you should consult an IFA that can search the market for the most suitable product for you.

1 Provide proof of income to the lender.

2 Organise an on-site survey and use the plans to assess the value.

3 Obtain mortgage offer, which is usually on a variable rate so the final mortgage can be checked to see if it is still the best offer researched. There may be a better version on the market nearer to completion.

4 If a freehold property, organise the insurance required before exchanging with the developer or gain separate cover.

5 Exchange contracts (when you pay over deposit or confirm the Exchange Bond).

6 Prior to completion, gain a snagging survey (see page 53) to confirm the property meets building regulation standards and has no problems, or highlights the problems.

7 Finalise your mortgage with your IFA.

8 Inform the developer of any snagging issues that need to be fixed.

9 Draw down mortgage monies.

10 Complete on the property and sell on to a new buyer or let out.

ONGOING FINANCES

- Gaining an off-plan mortgage. To exchange contracts with the developer you have to prove you have the finances available for the purchase.
- If you are buying a leasehold property or for some new-build developments, you may also have to finance a service charge, ground rent, buy-to-let fees and stamp duty.

LEGAL CHECKS

Most new-build contracts are not straightforward and are usually (understandably) in the developer's favour. For example, there may be clauses that bring forward the completion date with only six weeks' notice; not compensating for defects or, worse, if you have problems completing on time, even charge you interest!

It is important that your solicitor should fully understand your reasons for buying off-plan, so he or she can advise you accordingly. If you want to 'flip' the property and sell before completion,

> **"Your solicitor can only advise you properly if he or she understands your reasons for buying off-plan."**

you need a contract that is '**assignable**'. Make sure that your developer will accept this form of legal contract. Not all do as there is then no assurance that you will go ahead with the purchase and they may have to secure another buyer. If your developer isn't keen, see if you can use a less sensitive agreement that allows 'back-to-back' sales. With such an agreement, completion is assured for the developer but you are free to sell the property at completion time.

Some investors exchange on the rough layouts of off-plan properties and then exchange again with the final buyer. It is the final buyer who completes on the property with the developer, and for this you need to exchange with the assignable agreement.

If you are buying to let, check you are allowed to rent out the property and also who you can rent to as some developers exclude certain tenants, such as students or the Department of Health and Social Security (DHSS).

Jargon buster

Assignable contract Exchange contracts to buy the property on the understanding that you can sign over your agreement to buy the property to someone else for a different price

---

 For more information about snagging, go to www.inspectorhome.co.uk.

SNAGGING SURVEY

'Snagging' means describing defects in a new build and you should always have a professional snagging survey done prior to completion, which will cost £200–£500. According to statistics from 2002 to 2005, there are an average of eighty defects per new-build property. If you have an estate agent who you are buying from, ask him or her to attend when the survey is being done. Always keep a copy of the snagging list so that you can check that everything has been done.

There should be a legal clause in your purchasing contract to ensure that any defects revealed by such a survey are put right at the developer's expense and in a reasonable time frame. This is known as the defect period and it starts from the date of completion. Most developers let you know when the work will happen.

These surveys are important if you are investing in a buy-to-let property as you don't want complaints about the finish as soon as your tenants move in.

❝ The best time to sell is when prices have risen and there are few other rival properties on the market. ❞

UTILITY COMPANIES

Ask the developer which utility companies are supplying the site and whether and when you can change the provider(s). Changing a utility company can take weeks, so if you have a specific company that is offering you a better deal, make sure you have it written into the contract that you want it changed.

SELLING YOUR NEW BUILD

You can either sell your new build in the traditional way – through an estate agent or private advertising (see pages 78–81) – or by putting up notices at the development (with the agreement of the builder), either in windows or on boards. This is a way to advertise cheaply! Other routes are via private sales websites (see below) and even in the local post office.

Try to pick a good time to sell, ideally when there are few other properties on the market, and when prices have risen sufficiently to allow you the return you are looking for.

If you have a tenant installed, you will have to serve notice and sell once the property becomes vacant. If you find that you need to sell while the tenant is there, you could sell at auction or through investment websites. Make sure your legal documentation is in order so that the sale is not delayed.

 Private sale websites include www.houseweb.co.uk and www.propertybroker.co.uk.

Case Study — Bill and Imogen

Bill and Imogen have watched the property programmes and seen the hard work that renovating can incur and the problems with buy to let, so they have decided to look at buying off-plan and flipping. Their aim is to invest in property to gain a bigger deposit to buy a new property.

However, they rushed into their first purchase, buying through a company that 'finds' property deals and bought a property for £124,950, supposedly being valued at £147,000, giving a 15 per cent discount. They put down a 10 per cent deposit. However, when they came to sell eight months later, due to too many similar properties being on the market, they only achieved a sale price of £130,000.

Flat 1 (Sale price: £130,000)

Costs incurred	
Deposit	£12,495
Reservation fee	£1,000
Finder's fee (2.5%)	£3,125
Buying/selling costs	£4,500
Mortgage payments	– [1]
Service charges	– [1]
Total costs	**£21,120**
Total gross income [2]	**–£16,070**

[1] Flat 1 was sold before any mortgage/service charges were incurred
[2] Total gross income = £124,950 purchase price + £21,120 costs – £130,000 sale price = –£16,070

Rather than gaining money, Bill and Imogen lost over £16,000!

This case study shows that buying off-plan isn't as easy a way to gain money as it may at first appear. Getting any return in a slow or declining market is virtually impossible unless you gain a substantial discount. As a back-up plan, always check the rental potential so you can switch to letting the property for a period of time. However, this has different tax implications (see pages 202–6).

Renovating for profit

These days it seems as though everyone is jumping on the property renovation bandwagon. Some people are investors, others homeowners, but they all have the same goal – to spend money restoring and updating their properties.

Renovation considerations

It sounds simple: find a run-down property available at under its market value, make a few improvements plus a lick of paint and sell it on for a quick profit. But renovation is an increasingly competive and complicated process that can catch out inexperienced investors.

BE REALISTIC ABOUT YOUR FINANCES

The rewards of returning homes to their full glory – maybe a listed building or a sturdy Victorian terrace – are tremendous, but the most important reward for the investor is the financial one.

However, what was frequently a financial goldmine is now an increasingly difficult venture. Even long-term investors are struggling to find the ideal renovation project to make a profit on. Those doing it purely for investment purposes either buy properties when prices are low or buy at a discount. Consequently there is a move towards a mix of renovation and property development, such as buying a property with land and building one or more properties. Much depends on the amount of work required to make the property habitable but always bear in mind that 'profit' needs to take priority over 'renovating'. It is best to buy at a price that allows you to sell on with a 20 per cent profit on your initial investment after renovation costs.

Sellers can also stand in the way of your plans for 'easy money'. They are increasingly realising the potential of their properties and seek to maximise their own profits by holding out for the highest price. As a result, fewer sellers will accept discounted offers unless they are under enormous pressure to sell.

> **With a shortage of suitable renovation projects, there is a trend towards mixing renovation with property development.**

 For more information on health and safety issues to consider when renovating, see www.hse.gov.uk/pubns/indg411.pdf.

The pros and cons of investing in property renovation

Pros

- You can turn a profit within six months to a year.
- Work required can be minimal, for example a Halifax survey in 2006 suggests that decorating is the easiest way to increase a property's value.
- You gain a double benefit if you have bought in an area where the market is rising as well as by adding value. However, do not rely on a rising market to make a profit – property prices can fall, too.
- Property renovation can take advantage of tax breaks, such as savings on VAT and grants, to bring a property back to life and/or to make the building more energy efficient.
- Ability to renovate the property for a particular market.
- Satisfaction of turning a delapidated property into a beautiful home.

Cons

- It can be difficult to find the right property as too many people are competing to buy and do up for the long term. They are willing to pay more than an investor trying to make a profit in the short term.
- Cash investment is high compared to other property investments as you have to obtain a mortgage and cover the renovation costs.
- The market can turn against you during development. So if you buy with a six-month build in mind, prices may fall as you are trying to add value.
- Unknown problems can occur and drain cash profit. For example, you might find rotten timbers need replacing. Have between 10 and 30 per cent contingency in your budget.
- Planning permission and building regulations are tightening and this can delay or increase the cost of your project. Make sure you have the relevant certificates passing your work before you sell.
- Health and safety regulations will apply during renovation, so accident cover is absolutely essential (see insurance on pages 62–4).
- Theft of materials and equipment from the site can delay and increase the cost of your project. Make sure you are suitably insured (see also page 64).
- You only make your profit when you sell, but if you can't sell at the price you need, consider renting it until prices rise or demand increases.

Once you have secured the right property, it is imperative that you stick to your budget while developing the property for your target market. Most importantly, get the property finished and quickly back on the market.

Taking the figures in the table below as an example, if the renovation takes three months and the sale-to-completion process of the property a further three months, then the cost of the project overrunning by one month is:

£12,000/six months
= £2,000 per month

If the project overruns by three months, then your profit will be £41,670 – £6,000 = £35,670, and that reduces your profit by 14 per cent.

CONSIDER YOUR MARKET

Developing for the right market is critical in property renovation. The chart opposite shows the types of markets that you should be looking at.

If you have done your property renovation well and priced your property fairly within the market, you should gain an offer within six weeks and complete within a maximum of three months.

❝ Once you've bought the property, develop it quickly for your target buyer and get it back on the market. ❞

The potential value of a renovated property

Before putting in an offer you must fully cost your plans. If you discover at a late stage that the project is not financially worthwhile, you will have wasted valuable time and money, which could otherwise have been invested in something more viable.

	Example value/cost
What you can sell it for	£250,000
The cost of restoration	£25,000
Cost of funding the property during renovation	£12,000
Costs for buying and selling	£9,000
20% profit	£41,670
Price needed to secure the property	£162,330

Understanding your market

Type of market	Who to sell to	Type of renovation
Student market	• Buy-to-let investor. • Parent buying a home for offspring to share.	• Easy to clean and maintain internally and externally, so vinyl/laminate/tile flooring. • Kitchen/diner with lots of cupboard space; space for large fridge/freezer and washing/drying facilities; easy to change worktops/doors. • Separate toilet(s). • Possible room with en-suite; bathroom with bath and shower; shower with easy access to working parts.
Professional market	• Young professionals, male/female or two people looking to buy together.	• High quality trendy finish; hi-tech appliances; easy to maintain. • Use of outside space for entertaining/chilling, including at night. • Beautifully finished bathroom, ideally an en-suite shower/toilet. • Built-in storage space and parking space.
Family market	• People with new baby, with young children, or with older teenage children.	• Good finish, feeling of space and light. • Safety is important on stairs, in the garden, kitchen and bathroom. • Kitchen/diner with space for children and for parents. • Flooring easy to keep clean. • Bathroom with bath and shower (fitted with thermostat) preferably en-suite for parents/teenage room. • Easy-to-maintain garden, but grassed with room for play toys.
Period property	• Professional/older couple.	• Maintain, put back in and highlight period features. • Make sure any modern items, such as heating/kitchen appliances, complement the period features.

Finance and insurance

When a property is habitable, you take the conventional mortgage route. However, with renovation projects this may not be possible. There are three main types of property renovation and the type of project will determine how you can finance it.

BASIC RENOVATION

If the property is habitable and just needs updating, such as fitting a new kitchen and bathroom and flooring, together with painting and decorating, and you have spare cash, look for the most cost-effective mortgage on the open market. Ideally, look for good short-term mortgage deals that have little or no early redemption penalties. Your outgoing costs need to be as low as possible and when you sell, you can pay off the mortgage immediately.

STANDARD RENOVATION

This would typically require some building work and even planning approval. Don't forget, planning rules change, so permission may be refused even if, for example, a neighbouring property has already been extended. Check that the local planning department is happy with your proposals and exchange subject to planning approval.

This type of project may require a higher level of borrowing, so investigate specialist mortgages that pay out, preferably prior to doing the work, on a staged payment basis. This means you get the money only when you need it, thus avoiding unnecessary interest charges. For example, see the chart below.

It is possible to save a lot of money in interest payments by borrowing the funds required in stages.

Potential mortgage stage breakdowns

Stage	Funding required	Month required
Extension	£20,000	March
First fix	£10,000	May
Second fix	£5,000	June
Final fix	£3,000	July/August

MAJOR RENOVATION

This is where the property is uninhabitable, with quite possibly no running water or other utilities, no roof or other major structural problems and the property is unsafe. It may be a former commercial building. For this you need specialist finance (see overleaf), and, once again, staged payments can save you thousands of pounds.

Standard and major renovation projects will normally require purely specialist lenders if:

- Properties are uninhabitable, such as:
  - Barn conversion
  - Empty home with no kitchen/ bathroom facilities
  - Badly fire-damaged home.
- Lenders retain a portion of the funding, such as when:
  - Damp-proofing or timber treatment is required
  - Structural defects need to be corrected.

TYPES OF MORTGAGE

You can borrow money using your own home as security and if you intend to move in, you can do that as soon as the property is habitable. Then you can sell your previous home and pay off some or all of the debt, reducing your monthly outgoings. If you use the project itself as security, it is likely that there will be valuations at every stage (at a cost). Some mortgages or loans release the monies before each stage has been completed, others after each stage. To make your funds go further, it is worth looking at securing funding that releases the money upfront, as this allows you to use your own funds to pay out for costly time delays or unexpected bills.

Unlike owner-occupiers, who generally prefer repayment mortgages to ensure the house is theirs at the end of the term, property investors will sell on, so shouldn't need to pay off any of the capital. Mortgage interest payments are usually tax deductible (see pages 202–6) and interest-only mortgage payments are lower than repayment, so your cash outflow is reduced during the project.

Before making an offer, get a mortgage agreement in principle and then plan your finance in detail. You may need a 95 per cent mortgage or just a short-term loan, but either way getting the right funding and plans in place well in advance can save both time and money. If appropriate, it may be best for you to check out your strategy with an IFA, preferably one who has had previous experience of funding renovation projects.

For more information about different types of mortgages, see the *Which? Essential Guide* to *Buy, Sell and Move House.*

Applying for a loan

Before applying for a loan, obtain all the information that a specialist lender will require. This includes:

- Property details, such as the address.
- How much money you are investing in the property: both upfront and ongoing amounts.
- An independent survey from a surveyor who is experienced in property investment.
- List of all the works you plan to do.
- Budget, which gives detailed costings and timing of monies that you are requesting.
- Contingency fund for unexpected costs or if the property takes longer to sell than expected.
- Expected final sale price, ideally from the surveyor and/or local estate agents.

Once you have all this information, talk to an IFA or, alternatively, there are specialist companies that promote their financial services for this market.

Finding specialist lenders

The upside of using specialist registered mortgage advisers and IFAs to find a lender is that they have access to a wider range of financial products so are more likely to get your project funded – however dilapidated! As with all registered advisers, by law they have to give the best advice available.

The downside of using a specialist lender is that they are likely to cost more upfront for an arrangement fee. It can also be the case that the better the mortgage rate, the higher the arrangement fee, which could be up to 3.5 per cent of your mortgage.

INSURANCE FOR RENOVATION PROJECTS

As a minimum, most people buying a property with a mortgage have to have at least buildings insurance in place at exchange of contracts. The same is true for renovation projects, but the insurance required is much more complicated. You have a responsibility to have adequate cover and some insurance is a legal requirement. For example, if employing subcontractors on a labour-only basis (where you supply the materials), you need a minimum £5 million of employer's liability insurance.

❝ Specialists are more likely to get your project funded - for a price. ❞

For information on finding an IFA, go to pages 27-8. Companies that promote financial services for this market include www.buildstore.co.uk and www.assetz.co.uk.

If it's your own property and you already have buildings and contents insurance, check the position with your insurer. Will they still cover you if you decide to turn your property into a building site? And if something goes wrong while you are renovating, such as a waterproof cover blows off the roof and water gets in damaging the upstairs, will you be covered? Find out exactly what cover you have and whether it's what you need.

Types of insurance

There are various types of insurance to consider:

- **If you are buying a second property** and are leaving it empty, you need to insure the land/property but are also likely to need public liability cover.
- **Covering the building work** that is undertaken, for example from storm or flood damage, and ensuring against accidents that may affect the fabric of the building.
- **Public and employer's liability.** These are essential if you are managing the project yourself. If you are employing a builder and/or other tradespeople, get copies of both of their certificates and check with the insurance company that they are still valid.

- **Personal accident/death cover.** If you are doing the project yourself and need to cover the costs, even if you are ill or have an accident, this type of insurance may well pay dividends in a crisis.
- **On-site building materials and equipment.** Equipment and materials are expensive, so ensure that your valuables are secure and also make sure that both owned and hired equipment and even personal valuables are covered.
- **Buildings insurance.** It doesn't matter what is left of the building, or the state it is in. It is worth checking to see if you can get cover for the building, and if it subsides/gets burnt down, at least you will have some money with which to rebuild it.
- **Legal expenses.** Essential to cover any legal disputes with contractors or suppliers, or even the local authority.
- **Contents insurance.** If you are living in your renovation project at any point, then you will still need normal contents insurance for your own items such as electrical appliances, computers and furniture.

❝ Check what cover you already have and if it is what you need. ❞

 There are specialist mortgage lenders for some specific types of renovation, for example dedicated clubs such as the Thatched Owners Club (www.thatched-group.com/) and the Listed Owners Club (www.listedpropertyownersclub.co.uk).

One important consideration is to be sure that the property is still fully covered if it is to be left empty for a long period of time (weeks or more).

You can get insurance for a single property and short-term cover (anything from 6 to 18 months), which can be extended if necessary. Alternatively, you can take out an annual policy, which may be cheaper than individual ones if you have several or ongoing projects.

❝It might be cheaper to take out an annual policy if you run several projects.❞

Cost of insurance

Insurance can cost from £500 for six months on a small project to several thousand pounds for a major one. Costs vary according to the structure, size and value of the building as well as its state of dilapidation. Don't just go for the cheapest as accidents can be expensive – saving a few pounds could cost you thousands if things go wrong. Premiums can be reduced by offering to increase your excess, so check the position, and don't forget that the insurance is tax deductible.

Finding specialist renovation insurance

Check with a reputable IFA, but you can also try:

Magazines: *Build It, Home Building and Renovation, Move and Improve*

Shows: Property Investor, Home Building and Renovation, Grand Designs

Specialist insurance brokers: www.towergaterisksolutions.co.uk

Specialist insurers:
- www.buildstore.co.uk/finance/buildcare.html
- www.laplaya.co.uk/repairs_renovation.html
- www.periodproperty.co.uk
- www.renovationzone.com/
- www.self-builder.com/sb2/siteinsurance/quote.aspx

You can also visit the National Self Build and Renovation Centre in Swindon. Go to www.mykindofhome.co.uk for more information.

For more information on the tax implications of investing in property, see pages 202-6.

Find your project

Finding a renovation project that is profitable is getting harder every day. It can be disheartening if nothing within your budget makes financial sense.

In the past, it was rare to see a house for sale 'with detailed planning permission'. However, if the phrase is used today, it generally means that the seller is trying to make the money and there may not be enough profit in it for you. A property may also sell at auction for way over the guide price and again, when you consider the cost of it plus the cost of the work required, there would be no margin left when you sell on after renovation. Always bear in mind that all-important ideal goal of at least a 20 per cent profit.

WHAT SORT OF PROJECT IS RIGHT FOR YOU?

Unfortunately, just finding a renovation project is not enough to gain profit from renovation. You need to ask yourself if the property is suitable for your experience and contacts and, most importantly, can you take it on?

Apart from those already defined as 'basic', 'standard' and 'major' renovation projects there are many other possibilities. For example, within each level there are different property types, such as listed buildings, thatched properties, barn conversions or commercial buildings for adaptation

to residential units. Properties can be extended in all directions or split into flats. Your first consideration, therefore, is to decide what sort of project is right for you.

Do you have the experience for major renovation?

'Part-time' renovators must realistically decide how many hours/days/weeks/months they can spend while still in a full-time job. Unless you employ a project manager or delegate the job to a trusted member of the renovation team, you must be there as project manager when crucial decisions are required, and not at work or on holiday when you should be ordering materials and sorting out problems. You are likely to be investing

❝It is not just a question of a finding a renovation project: it has to be one suitable for your skills, level of experience and contacts. ❞

a great deal of money in the project, perhaps even more than your annual salary, so don't risk losing all your hard-earned cash, make sure you have a good team working with you.

Unless you have experience of working with builders and suppliers, and are low on funds, experience and time, it may be better to cut your teeth on a basic renovation project. Eventually you will have the money to take on bigger projects – and be able to afford the expert help you will need.

If, however, you already have the funds you need for professional help, a lack of experience doesn't mean you can't take on a major renovation. You will need a good builder, though, as well as a trusted and knowledgeable project manager. It is imperative that you check every decision that is made at each stage and continue to seek advice throughout the project.

You can also employ a local consultant, such as a retired builder or architect, who doesn't want to be involved on a day-to-day basis but who will give help and advice as required.

66 Starting with basic renovation projects brings experience and funds for bigger schemes. **99**

WHERE TO LOOK

Seeking a property to renovate can seem like looking for a needle in a haystack at times. There will always be the one that got away: the 'perfect' project that falls apart because the costs would be too high, because someone else got there first, or because it wasn't as good as you first imagined it might be. And that's if you have even found something to look at in the first place. However, those with tenacity and the right kind of information can and eventually will get the break they need.

When you start hunting for property renovation projects, it's important to understand that viewing one or two properties isn't enough to find a gem of a deal and you need to search for at least 50 property opportunities. Visit the ones that seem to stack up financially and then narrow these down to five to ten properties. Consider them in detail and make offers on one or more to ensure that you get the deal that will return a profit.

Internet property portals

The internet and portals (see box, opposite) show what properties are available, their specifications and how prices vary by type and area. These sites are helpful as they show what sort of properties are for sale and how quickly they sell. If you find a property that looks appealing from a renovation perspective, it is worth seeing what else someone could buy with a similar specification within a three-mile radius – as most buyers will move within this area.

Work out what the property might sell for once it is done up – and if there is a margin to be made.

Local media

Local newspapers, including free ones, and publications such as *Daltons Weekly* and *Loot*, are a great source of information about properties for sale. Sometimes they also feature renovation projects that have, or are about to, come on the market.

Estate agents

Most estate agents have properties on their books that are ripe for renovation, but they are often priced quite high and there are unlikely to be many major projects, unless the agent specialises in them. In rural areas, for example, try looking for your empty barn by targeting the agent who sells agricultural lots, as he or she may already know farmers who want to sell.

Start a relationship with the agents by meeting them face-to-face and tell them what you're looking for. Ensure they recognise that you are realistic about pricing, know what you are doing and that you have the funds available, particularly if they find something they need a quick deal on. Move quickly on viewings and if you make sure the offer is fair and not something the agent would be embarrassed to put to his or her client.

> **"Meet agents face-to-face and build relationships so that they know you are serious."**

Auction houses

Guide prices at auctions may seem to be low, but remember that they are set to attract as many people as possible. Popular and attractive opportunities will be a focus for competitive bidding, which drives up prices, confounding the long-held view that prices are always lower at auction. They can be great places to bag a bargain, but check out the property and market beforehand and don't get carried away!

If you offer to buy a property that you then find you can't afford to buy, you will lose your deposit, which is 10 per cent of the purchase price. Clearly this could be a great deal of money. Follow the steps outlined overleaf to make sure you are not caught out at an auction.

On average, 24 per cent of the properties at an auction don't get sold. If 'your' lot fails to sell as it doesn't reach the reserve price or you get no bids, ask the auctioneer afterwards if it is possible to do a deal.

 For property portals go to www.rightmove.co.uk or www.findaproperty.co.uk. The website for *Loot* is www.loot.com and that for *Daltons Weekly* is www.daltons.co.uk.

Steps to buying at auction

1 Visit an auction without buying anything, to gain a feel for what happens.

2 Talk to the auctioneer about costs involved as a buyer, whether they have renovation projects coming up regularly, how much these are going for above the guide price and areas that might have properties within your budget.

3 Consider signing up to an auction subscription site, such as www.eigroup.co.uk, to see the types of properties that are coming through. Think about where in the country you are most likely to find the type of renovation project you want, at a budget that you can afford and within a day's travelling.

4 Source your finance and gain a mortgage agreement in principle.

5 Look at as many properties as possible. Consider 50-100 properties, if there are that many, and if there are fewer than that, consider every one on offer. Make a checklist and cost out each one.

6 Narrow down the properties to between five and ten and pay a builder or surveyor to check them prior to the auction. Give them your calculations and lists of things to do and ask them to check that your costings are accurate.

7 Look at the legal situation, particularly if there are issues with flats and leasehold properties or planning. See also whether there are any legal restrictions to your plans, particularly if it involves party walls (a shared wall in a terraced or semi-detached house).

8 With the help of your surveyor and/or estate agent, work out the minimum and maximum price you would expect to get for the property. Taking the minimum price, assess your likely profit margin and see if it makes financial sense.

9 Before going to the auction:

- Check the property is still available.
- See if the vendor will accept an offer prior to the auction and take it off the market.
- Make sure that your deposit is easily accessible – remember they don't take cash, but do take cheques as long as you have proof that the money is in the relevant account.
- Organise the relevant insurance cover (see pages 62–4).
- If you can't make it on auction day, get someone to take your bids by phone. It is, however, better if you can be there in person.

10 On auction day:

- Take along ID, such as a passport/driving licence and personal gas or electricity bills (with your own name and address printed on them). You need these to confirm an offer.
- Get to the auction early; make sure you are seated in viewing distance of the auctioneer.
- Check the 'addendum' sheets for any last-minute changes.

11 If making a bid:

- Attract the auctioneer's attention, and once you have this he or she will come back to you.
- Bid on the right lot; it is not that difficult to buy the wrong property in error!

12 If your bid is successful:

- Hand over a 10 per cent deposit.
- Sign the memorandum of sale.
- Give the auction house your insurance policy details.

13 Contracts are exchanged immediately and you then have 28 days to complete on the sale or you will lose your deposit.

Specialist subscription services

There are many internet and even fax or mailing services that will offer 'thousands' of property opportunities at the click of a button. However, buyer beware! Any subscription service is only as good as the people who are running it. The lists of properties 'available' could be weeks or months, even years, out of date. Ideally, you want to look at subscription sites that allow you to:

- **Call them to talk about their services** and preferably speak to someone rather than an answering machine.
- **Ask them questions,** such as those given in the box below.
- **Have a free one- or two-week trial.**
- **Have a money-back guarantee.**
- **Ask how much it costs** and are fees paid monthly, quarterly or yearly?

&&Buyer beware! Any subscription service is only as good as the people who are running it, so make plenty of checks.

If you can, sign up for a short time to start with. If it works for you, then join for longer and try to get the benefit of an annual discount. Whatever route you take, always check when and how to cancel the subscription and make sure there are no penalties for doing so.

If these sites are good, they can help you to research different properties and types of renovation projects, and work out where to search for what you want.

Questions to ask a subscription service

By asking a subscription site the following questions you will glean a good deal more information about how it is run and how reliable it should be.

1 How many properties are for sale, in your area, right now?

2 Who inputs the information, the owner or the company?

3 How regularly do you check the properties are still for sale?

4 How do you check? By email? By telephone?

 Sites that can help you find property renovation projects include: www.barnsetc.co.uk/, www.plotfinder.net, www.plotsearch.co.uk and www.renovatealerts.com/.

They may cost from £10 a month to as much as £400 for a full year but, as with other costs, these can sometimes be deducted from any profit you make.

Organisations that sell property stock

It is likely that most organisations with property to sell will do so either through an agent or at auction. This is to prove to the business that they are getting the best possible price. In some cases, they may have no choice but to dispose of a property in this way.

Organisations that you can approach include your local housing association, council and even local or national mortgage lenders who may have repossessed properties that they would like to dispose of quickly. Some religious organisations sell off old churches, halls or properties, so it may be worth contacting them too. The National Trust also puts properties that they no longer require on the market.

Not all organisations will be happy to deal with you directly, but if they have anything available, ask if you can view the property. Take measurements and have tradespeople cost any renovation work that you may want to do.

Some of the property stock sold by organisations come with complicated legal restrictions. For example, properties around churches can have 'chancel repairs' attached to them, which means that you would be responsible for the upkeep of the local church building.

Get out and about

Another really good way of finding a property to renovate, especially if you know the area you want, is literally to get out and about in the car, or even on foot, to search. Look out for properties that appear to be empty and in need of repair.

It may be that many people you contact are being spoken to on a regular basis, so don't expect them to be grateful – they may be fed up with the calls! However, to find a suitable deal that stacks up from a profitable perspective you may have to try every conceivable route you know.

> **❝ Get out and about in your car or on foot, seeking out properties to renovate; especially if you know the area you want to develop in. ❞**

There are other organisations that can you help you find empty properties and their owners. These include www.emptyhomes.com/, www.empro.co.uk/ and www.propertyrenovate.com/company.htm, although the latter two sites tend to be more biased towards London.

Viewing and surveying

Once you start viewing properties, it is essential to make sure that you have a checklist of requirements to record as much as possible. You will also need to organise a survey of your chosen property.

THE FIRST VIEWING

On a first viewing, you rarely see all the faults with a property, so start by making a quick checklist of what to look for, such as the roof, chimneys, external walls, lighting and decoration.

THE SECOND VIEWING

You are more likely to notice other details on a second viewing. Make sure that you:

- **Create a drawing of the property's layout** so you can think through the changes that could be made.
- **On the drawing highlight which walls are load bearing** so you know what can't be changed.
- **Make a list of all the work to be done** either by room or by task.
- **Take measurements of areas** you think you may want to alter.
- **Take any tradespeople with you** to cost and quote for the work.
- **Visit local agents** to look at comparable properties and check what the property might sell for.

- Find out the level of interest in the **property** and if the vendor has turned down any offers.
- **Ask agents what the demand for the type of property is,** and how many buyers they have on their books.

Once you have viewed the property look through the property portals on the internet again, and find out what price similar properties are being sold for rather than what they are being marketed at. Then you will have an idea what you might get for your property.

OBTAINING A SURVEY

If you are keen to make an offer on a property, and it's a standard or major renovation or an unusual building, such as a listed building, it may be a worthwhile investment to get a survey done first to make sure that you have considered all the issues. Don't forget that survey costs can be deducted from any profit. If you know the surveyors well or can build a rapport with them, they

For more information on what to be aware of at a first viewing, go to www.designsonproperty.co.uk.

Example budget plan

	Month 1				Month 2					Budget total
Week	1	2	3	4	1	2	3	4	5	
General building work										
Prepare outside foundations										
Take down kitchen wall										
Build new kitchen wall										
Sub-total cost	£600	£600	£400	£750						£2,350
Plumbing and electrics										
First fix electrics										
First fix plumbing										
Sub-total cost					£750	£600				£1,350
Kitchen re-fit										
Fit new kitchen										
Tile kitchen floor										
Tile rest of kitchen										
Sub-total cost							£1,000	£800	£400	£2,200
Plumbing and electrics										
Second fix electrics										
Second fix plumbing										
Sub-total cost								£300	£250	£550
Total	£600	£600	£400	£750	£750	£600	£1,000	£1,100	£650	£6,450

may be able to do a cheaper, basic survey before you make an offer. Once the offer is accepted, you will start incurring legal and financial fees.

BUDGET ACCURATELY

It is essential to spend time preparing a budget for your project. Borrow money only as and when you have to and at the

For more information on building regulations that apply for individual projects, go to www.planningportal.gov.uk and especially www.planningportal.gov.uk/england/genpub/en/1115314762582.html.

best available rate. Try never to borrow on credit cards or get emergency loans as they are an expensive and potentially ruinous way of obtaining funds.

Plan from start to finish

Do this by using either an ordinary spreadsheet or special project planning and estimation software (see below). Budget plans (see page 73) can be done either room by room, if a basic renovation, or by job and stage.

As well as setting out what needs doing and when, estimate when you will need to pay for materials. For example, if you have an account with a supplier, you may need to order on 1 May for delivery on 1 June, but don't need to pay until 1 July.

Involve your surveyor

If you have already had a survey done, the surveyor will hopefully have submitted a cost for the necessary work. If not, it may be worth contacting them for a ballpark figure. Your biggest challenge is probably getting an accurate quote for labour and materials. Asking for a detailed quote involving one or two days' work by a tradesperson is sometimes a tall order! You can help by:

- Making a detailed list of the work required and breaking it down in to labour and materials.

You can get help

Some suppliers, such as Jewson and Build Centre, have specialist help available for renovation projects provided that the spend is in tens of thousands of pounds. Sign up with companies such as www.buildstore.co.uk/materials/ and they will take plans for large renovation projects, which include extensions, and, sometimes free of charge, provide estimates for costs and materials.

Bespoke software systems, such as www.estimators-online.com, will independently cost your project for an average fee of around £100. However, they may estimate a builder at £125 a day when in your area it may be nearer £160, or the quote for a standard kitchen may not match your desire for a bespoke one, so check the results carefully against your own specifications.

- Estimating how many days the work might take.
- Requesting a quote for each job with a final price, which should be fixed.
- Asking for a recommended contingency budget for the job.
- Ensuring you apply for any planning or building regulations required.

For more information on project planning and estimation software, go to www.hbxl.co.uk/ and www.quantiquote.co.uk/.

Managing the renovation

Many first-time property renovators are convinced it will save money if they do the work themselves. This is rarely the case, unless the individual is a fully qualified tradesperson.

FINDING THE RIGHT PERSON FOR THE JOB

Unless properly qualified, there are also legal rules that make it impossible for you to do much of the work involved, notably gas, glazing and electrical jobs, for which building regulations have been tightened over recent years. These all have to be carried out, or at least signed-off, by a qualified person.

Project manager

If you have a substantial renovation project and are in full-time work, it is preferable to employ a project manager or building contractor. Although it will cost you more money in the short term, a well-organised project manager should ensure that first-class tradespeople are employed. These will turn up on time, do the work to a high standard and charge what they originally quoted. A good project manager can cost around £350 per day, but will save you time and/or money through his or her knowledge of materials and contacts.

Tradespeople

When looking for tradespeople, there are various ways of finding them. One of the best ways is to find someone else who has had similar work done and is happy to recommend their builders. Building companies usually have access to all the necessary trades, such as electricians, plasterers, plumbers, painters and decorators. You may pay a premium for this service but it may be worthwhile your peace of mind. Another route would be to employ subcontractors on an individual basis. The downside is that you will be responsible for the individual contracts, each subcontractor turning up on time and sticking to their quote.

> **" A good project manager knows first-class tradespeople who turn up on time and charge what they quoted. "**

 To find out more information about project managers, go to www.apm.org.uk.

DIY OR GSI?

An important part of any 'renovation for profit' project is understanding the real costs of 'doing it yourself' (DIY) versus 'getting someone in' (GSI). This seems to be a case of 'time' versus 'money' but it isn't that clear cut. For example, if you decide to clear a property yourself, it may take you two days to do. However, if you employ someone who does it for a living, it may only take a day and cost around £200. If instead of clearing the property you can use these two days to get your time plan and budgeting correct, which gives you the best value for money?

Even if you are not a qualified tradesperson, you can take on some work if you have had some experience – this includes decorating, tiling and interior design. Other work such as plastering, structural building work, carpentry, electrics, gas, and fitting kitchens and bathrooms, are likely to be done more quickly – and to a better standard – by the professionals than if you do it yourself.

When deciding whether to DIY or GSI when you are renovating for profit, you should consider the following points with each job:

- **Will the professional do it faster than you**? You can offset their costs against the time it takes you to get the property back on the market.

- **How can you best get the professional finish** required for your type of renovation project?
- **Are you legally allowed to do the work?**
- **Is it more cost-effective for you to source the materials** – or ask the tradesperson to purchase them for you?

In some cases it may be better to employ a skilled professional, but organise and purchase the materials yourself. Always request a detailed quote from a tradesperson that allows you to see their labour and detailed materials costs separately. You can then check to see if they are buying the same kind of materials that you would.

❝ Even if you employ a professional, buy the materials yourself. ❞

LETTERS OF AGREEMENT AND CONTRACTS

Once you have decided on what jobs are better for you to do and which are more suited to the professionals, it is important to ensure that you and the builder/tradesperson have a legal agreement. This may be set out in a letter, but ideally would be an official contract.

 There are many trade associations you can turn to for local experts in different skills. See the websites in Useful addresses on page 213.

Letter of agreement

A letter of agreement should include:

- A description of the work to be done and a price for it.
- Confirmation of who does what and their qualifications.
- Information about how the work will be paid for and when.
- Details of start and finish dates.
- What happens if there are increases in project costs or if there is a dispute.

Contract

A contract sets out a proper legal framework for the job and allows you to fall back on the law if there are any disputes. Make sure you always check a contract carefully before signing it. It may be worth having it checked over by a solicitor before making it legally binding. Information that should be included in a contract includes:

- Full details of the contractor, including his or her address and contact details (office and mobile phone numbers), and registration and/or VAT particulars if applicable.
- A detailed description of the work to be carried out.
- The cost of the work and an agreement to advise you if there are any increases before going ahead.
- Details of any labour or materials that you may be supplying yourself.
- Confirmation that the work will comply with all legal requirements and that the necessary certificates will then be issued on completion.

- Start and finish times and dates.
- Details of the contractor's insurance for employer's and public liability.
- Details of what recourse you have, including agreed compensation levels, if there are problems, including overrunning on dates or the work not being up to standard.
- How payment will be made and under what circumstances payments can be withheld.
- How disputes will be resolved if agreement can't be reached.

Both parties should have a signed copy of the contract. Attached to it should be any relevant documents, such as building plans and specifications, copies of the appropriate building regulations, copies of insurance documents, guarantees that will apply to the work being carried out and any certificates required, such as for gas safety.

For peace of mind always take the time and trouble to get these agreements in place and legally watertight before you start your project. If you don't, you will almost certainly regret it. Invest in getting it right and you could save yourself a lot of money in the event of things going wrong or many sleepless nights worrying what to do about it.

❝A contract allows you to fall back on the law if there are any disputes.❞

Selling the property

Before you even start your renovation project, you should have identified and talked to estate agents who sell the particular type of property you are renovating to gain information on 'dos' and 'don'ts' regarding the finish and expenditure.

RESEARCH ESTATE AGENTS

If you haven't already been tracking which agents are selling the type of property you are renovating, then as soon as you start the project make sure you do so. Read the property papers on a weekly basis. Note down similar properties within a three-mile radius of yours and see how long they take to sell. When they do, talk to the sales agent and ask if they can give you an idea on the final selling price.

On average, 80 per cent of buyers move within three miles, so look for properties similar to yours and the agents they sell through. You should be able to find three to four agents that have experience of selling the kind of property you are creating and concentrate only on those agents who are actually selling rather than those who have properties 'for sale'.

Some agents try to offer high valuations to gain a vendor's business, so properties that are still for sale after two months or more are usually far from helpful as a comparison. Their inflated prices bear no relation to selling prices and will give you unreal expectations, which should be ignored.

When you are deciding which agency should market your property, make sure that they:

- **Have sold properties** that are similar to yours within the last three to six months.
- **Are members of an organisation** such as the National Association of Estate Agents (NAEA), Royal Institution of Chartered Surveyors (RICS) and/or Ombudsman for Estate Agents (OEA).
- **Have buyers already on their books** looking for your type of property.
- **Can guarantee a certain number of viewings** within the first four to six weeks.
- **Will promote your property** by direct mail, online, in the local press on a weekly basis and in the agent's window. Don't forget you need to sell quickly and for a profit, not just 'sell when you can'.
- **Are willing to negotiate a deal** based on the selling price – the higher the selling price, the more commission they will earn.
- **Will keep you up to speed** on a weekly basis with regard to the

number of viewings, second viewings and offers.

- **Will check the viability of each potential purchaser,** from being able to afford the property to seeing how quickly they can move from offer to completion.
- **Provide accurate and enticing** property particulars.
- **Will advise you on a weekly basis** of the progress of the sale from offer through to completion.

Also check:

- How the property will be marketed.
- Who will do the viewings (ideally they should do the first, you the second).
- How they screen and follow-up on potential buyers.
- Who in the agency will look after you and update you on progress.
- What are their terms and conditions (your solicitor should check them)?
- If they don't gain an offer in six weeks – can you move to another agent?
- How do they handle complaints?

> **❝There is rarely one price for a property: it depends how fast you want to sell. ❞**

GET A VALUATION

Once you have identified the 'selling' agents then ask them to come round to look at and value the property. If you haven't done so before, show them your plans and an idea of what the finished property will look like. Explain the market you are going for and first check with them at what price they would market the property. If you have an idea at this stage, you can share with them the level at which you have to sell in order to make a profit. Ask whether your figures are realistic, if they think your renovation plans are the right ones and if they have any other suggestions.

Many people think a property is worth just one price. This is rarely the case, particularly with renovated properties. Any agent worth their salt will be able to give you three prices, and back up their recommendations with similar properties they have recently sold. The three prices are:

- **Asking price:** what the property should be marketed at in agents windows/the press/online.
- **Six-week sale price:** in order to maximise your profit, you want to turn around the offer to completion process in three months maximum and to do this you need to have an offer within six weeks.

Relevant estate agent organisations are the National Association of Estate Agents (www.naea.co.uk), the Royal Institution of Chartered Surveyors (www.rics.org.uk) and the Ombudsman for Estate Agents (www.oea.co.uk).

- **Two-week sale price:** just in case your money gets tied up in the property, it's best to know what is a 'cracking' sale price that will guarantee you an offer within two weeks.

> **❝ If you market early while work is still going on, make sure the agent only sends viewers who can see past the 'mess' of ongoing renovation. ❞**

WHEN TO MARKET YOUR PROPERTY

When selling your property you have two choices on when to market. If it's a basic renovation, it may be worth seeing if you could start promoting the property to buyers already on the agent's list.

Marketing early

Viewers tend to split into two – the first group can see past your 'mess' and have a good idea of what the property will look like when you have finished. The second will not be able to. So if you decide to market early, then make sure that the agent only allows viewings to those clients who they know well and who can see beyond half-plastered or half-painted walls.

The advantage of marketing early is that you can exchange prior to finishing, getting some guarantee of a deposit prior to the end of the build. The added advantage is that if you finish when promised at the time of exchange, you can move to completion within a matter of weeks, rather than waiting for a buyer and then taking months to exchange and complete.

The negative points of marketing early are twofold:

- People can't see the value you are adding mid project and, as a result, offer too low a price.
- You can get caught in renovating the property to their tastes, rather than to what you had planned. Unless you have exchanged at the time you 'bespoke' the property to the vendor, then you could end up in the worst position – you develop to an individual's tastes and then lose them as a buyer and struggle to sell the property on to another buyer.

If you do get a buyer early and adapt your renovation to their tastes, make sure that the deposit is big enough to compensate you for changing the property back to your original plans if it all falls through.

 To research historical and latest property price information, go to www.hometrack.co.uk and www.landregistry.gov.uk/houseprices.

Holding on too long

Unlike when you are selling for yourself, there is a cost to 'holding' a property, such as mortgage, insurance, council tax and utility bills. This could run into hundreds or thousands of pounds a month. It is always better to lose a few thousand pounds than to hang out for months for a 'top' price that may never materialise. If your ongoing costs are £1,500 per month, it may be better to accept an offer that is £3,000 below what you wanted, knowing that you can sell and bank the profit two months faster. The alternative is to hold on for a better offer, but meanwhile every month that you don't complete, the costs will be eating in to the profit that you would originally have made.

If the property is ready, it may even be worth putting it into auction to gain a quick sale. There are many buy-to-let investors, for example, looking for properties that tenants can move into immediately. This could be the quickest and most profitable way for you to take the money from your project.

If, however, you are struggling to sell your property at the price you need, check to see how much you could gain by renting it out instead. This is a good second option if the market is poor or buyers are just not biting. You can sign up to short-term lets from a minimum of three to six months and help to cover your costs while keeping the property on the market. Or rent it out, remortgaging for your next project and sell in a year's time when the market is better.

> **❝ There is a high cost on 'holding' a property to try to get the highest price. Accepting a lower offer could save you money. ❞**

Be realistic about the price of your property

Understanding how much to market your property for is critical. Yes, the agents will have a view, as should your surveyor, and it's worth getting the latter back in to value it for you when he or see can see the final finish.

There is always a temptation when you have put your heart, soul and hard-earned cash into a project to then price it as high as you can. This is probably the biggest mistake that first-time investors make. Unless you are marketing to really exclusive individuals, it's much better to price the property lower than the average on the market, get lots of interest and then hopefully get an offer near or at your target price.

Case Study   Jack

Jack couldn't afford to buy a property to move into straightaway in the area he wanted or even surrounding areas, so he turned to looking at property auctions and saw a property that he could afford - a flat above a shop. Unfortunately, he hadn't seen the property or even had a survey done and underestimated renovation costs. As a result, he lost money. He did get to live in the property for a minimal cost, but didn't make enough to be able to afford the property that he wanted.

Jack bought the flat for £119,000, so it was under the stamp duty threshold and he renovated the property while living in it over a 12-month period. His buying and selling costs were £4,910 and he put down a 5 per cent deposit of £5,950. The mortgage costs were around £6,500 for the year.

Jack's renovation costs included:

Labour (electrics and plumbing)	£950
Materials	£1,550
Kitchen	£2,500
Bathroom	£1,000
Total	**£6,000**

He then sold the property 12 months later for £135,000.

Jack's investment was £17,410 (including mortgage payments) and he received:

£135,000 proceeds - £119,000 purchase cost - £17,410 expenses
= -£1,410 loss.

Having sold the property quite quickly, if Jack had made a profit he may be subject to taxation even though he has lived in the property (see pages 202–6), so this would need to be checked out first.

To have made money, Jack should have costed-out the project properly and re-calculated the figures based on a 10 per cent and 30 per cent overspend to check they still added up. He could also have reduced the costs of the bathroom and kitchen by negotiating better, or looking for cheaper deals. Finally, adding up all those 'additional materials' was a big cost that hadn't been catered for and a contingency would have helped to have covered these.

Buy-to-let residential

Buy to let has been seen over the last few years as an investment opportunity that is not to be missed, something anyone can do with little or no professional guidance. If only the reality matched the hype!

Why buy to let?

One important aspect of buy to let is that it is not something that normally involves a quick return. It should be considered a minimum five-year investment plan and ideally you should be involved for no less than 10–15 years on each property. This time span means you can generally ride out the ups and downs of the property and rental markets.

People get involved in buy to let for many different reasons, some purely accidental. Maybe they were unable to sell in a poor market and, needing to move on, ended up renting out the property instead. If this happened in the early 1990s, for example, the good returns since would have enabled them to reinvest in more properties, and ultimately they could have ended up with a whole property portfolio. Other people have property left to them or buy in a favourite holiday area and need to cover costs for non-holiday periods, but whatever the reason, the end result is the same – they are now landlords, with all the responsibilities that that involves.

With such advertisements as 'Build a portfolio in a year and become a property millionaire' in the press, it can

The pros and cons of buy to let

Pros

- If you buy wisely, someone else will cover all the ongoing costs of your investment.
- If you plan your legal and tax positions well, most of your capital gains could be cash profit.
- It is possible to get a good, steady income if you buy at a real discount and always have good tenants.

Cons

- It is a long-term investment, ideally a minimum of 5–15 years.
- Time investment is high, such as renewing tenants, checking inventories and legal agreements or fixing burst pipes.
- Bad tenants may not pay and have to be evicted, which could take six months or more, and any damage done has to be paid for.
- You have to pay out money to cover costs when there is no tenant or costs rise above tenant income.

Buy-to-let returns in 2007

Below is a summary of the average returns from buy-to-let investors according to Paragon Mortgages.

Average yield (based on average rental income achieved of £11,300 per year) 6 per cent
Capital growth (based on average property prices of £187,000) 15.3 per cent
Total annual returns (based on yield and capital growth) 21.3 per cent

Ideally, when you are investing in a buy-to-let property, you would want to outperform other income generating investments by the average yield of 6 per cent and your capital growth to outperform general housing market performance and other capital generating investments such as stocks/shares. A year-on-year growth of 15 per cent compares to 8.1 per cent growth in average house prices in England and Wales according to the www.landregistry.gov.uk.

To keep up to date with monthly buy-to-let performance, visit the news and press section on www.paragon-mortgages.co.uk and www.arla.co.uk.

be very tempting to think that you can build a portfolio and give up your job. However, such advertisements are almost certainly too good to be true (see the box, above).

According to the Association of Residential Letting Agents, the average buy-to-let investor has six properties. Profits can vary widely but assuming an annual average of £2,000 from each property the resulting income of £12,000 is probably not the sort of retirement income you had in mind. To acquire even the average UK salary of £28,000 would require building a portfolio of properties worth around £2.6 million. For this, your cash investment would be £390,000 (the minimum 15 per cent deposit required) and, in addition, you would need a large contingency fund for ongoing maintenance, unexpected costs and voids.

THE DIFFERENT TYPES OF BUY TO LET

It is hard work finding a property that gives a good financial return, looking for and after tenants and fixing things that go wrong. Before you start, you must spend time working out where to invest your money and in what, assessing your objectives and doing it all in the most tax-efficient way. None of this is easy or quick, and is certainly not for the faint-hearted.

Whatever type of buy to let you choose, you must buy at a discounted price of 10 per cent or more to cover your buying and selling costs, and make sure that current demand will last for the length of your planned investment. This is generally a minimum of 15 years, and you should look for more information by studying local authority plans and talking to local employers and letting agents.

85

Professional buy to let

You can let through companies, for example, to senior managers, for as short a period as three months. Everything should be provided, for example, bedding and crockery, and utility bills should be included in the rent. Alternatively, you can let your property for the standard time of six months or more through companies, relocation agents or to private tenants. Schools, transport, communications and city-centre living may be important to professional people or families so if these are your markets, buy in the right areas. For the pros and cons of professional buy to lets, see below.

❝Look into the university's plans. Are they intending to grow? Will they build more accommodation? ❞

Student buy to let

As more students go to university the opportunities for buy to let in this market have increased. Parents have invested in this market to keep down costs by renting out additional rooms and hopefully to sell at a profit at the end of their child's course.

If you are interested, look at whether the university is continuing to grow and attract new students. Find out if they have plans to build more of their own accommodation. Are the majority of students local, and so can live at home, or from some distance away, even overseas? You also need to consider whether you let the rooms separately (potentially making it a home in multiple occupation, see opposite) or under one tenancy agreement, which may be easier but provide a lower return.

One area that many landlords do forget is marketing specifically to the mature university market, such as postgraduate students and current or

---

The pros and cons of professional buy to let

Pros	Cons
• Rents may be higher than average.	• To get a high rent, the specifications must be high, so usually costs more to bring up to standard.
• Companies may be paying the rent rather than individual tenants.	• The shorter letting periods mean there is a higher chance of voids, which can quickly negate any investment returns.
• You can get fixed long-term rents if you work closely with companies who offer temporary placements/ contracts to workers.	• Longer-term lets mean more updating and renovating.

The pros and cons of a student buy to let

Pros	Cons
• Willingness of tenants to live in cheaper and more basically renovated properties.	• This market is 'over supplied' in some areas, reducing returns.
• Higher rental return by letting out most of the rooms as bedrooms.	• You are competing not only with other landlords, but high quality purpose-built accommodation from property developers.
• According to mortgage supplier HBOS, 'the average house price in the top 20 university cities and towns trades at a premium of £48,020 to the average house price in their region'.	• May require annual refurbishment.
	• May not pay out rental income outside of term time.

visiting staff, who may make more suitable tenants. For the pros and cons of student buy to lets, see above.

Homes in multiple occupation (HMO)

The definition of a licensed HMO is a property of three or more habitable storeys (including attics or basements), which is occupied by five or more people who are not all in the same family and who share some communal rooms. The Association of Residential Letting Agents (ARLA) estimates that 6 per cent of rented properties are classed as HMOs. If you let to students or migrant workers and there are more then five people in a three-storey property, for example, it is likely to be classed as an HMO in which case you will need to purchase a licence.

The pros and cons of HMOs

Pros	Cons
• Yields can be good, giving on average 8-9 per cent compared to 5-6 per cent for standard lets.	• Constantly having to re-let individual rooms and being liable for keeping up with current legislation such as fire regulations.
• Demand could also increase with the arrival of more migrant workers.	• You are also responsible for paying the council tax, although you can claim that back in the rent.
• HMOs can be sold on with planning permission to turn them back in to large houses or flats, increasing potential profits.	

HMOs in Scotland and Northern Ireland

The laws in Scotland and Northern Ireland for HMOs are different from those in England and Wales and can be summarised as follows:

In Scotland: all residential property that is rented out to three or more unrelated tenants in Scotland has to be licensed as an HMO. Local authorities issue a licence only after an they have undertaken an inspection to check that properties meet certain basic standards, and these licences are then valid for a year.

In Northern Ireland: there is a statutory registration scheme for all HMOs – all properties capable of housing more than ten people must be registered by a person associated with the property. Gas, electrical and fire safety considerations are important requirements. Properties housing two or fewer families are excluded from the scheme.

These are issued by the local authority and cost between £300 and £1,100 a year. There may be a reduction if you belong to specialist landlord schemes. For the pros and cons of HMOs, see page 87.

Holiday lets

You can see these purely as a financial investment or as a property for holidays or retirement in the future, and you may wish to break even or make a profit. If holidays are your priority, check out the cost over 10–15 years of a two to three week holiday each year compared to buying and selling a property in the UK or abroad. Whatever you decide, take specialist holiday let legal and tax advice before proceeding. Holiday homes that are let out to others are complicated and

to be classed as a 'holiday let' to take advantage of tax relief they need to meet the following criteria:

- Be in the UK.
- Make the let available for a minimum of 140 days each year.
- Not let to the same person for 31 or more days in a seven-month period.
- Let the property for income for 70 or more days annually.

Importantly, ascertain potential income and find out how long the 'holiday season' is – the longer the better. In some places abroad (Bulgaria, for example), the season is incredibly short. You need to be looking at a minimum of 20–30 weeks rental per year and the

 For more information about HMOs and other buy to lets, go to www.communities.gov.uk /housing/rentingandletting/privaterenting/. To get a licence, contact your local authority. For information specifically about HMOs in Scotland, go to www.scotland.gov.uk and for Northern Ireland, go to www.nihe.gov.uk/hmos.

cost of the property should be better value than the average local hotel.

You should also compare the **yield** and **capital growth** potential of a holiday buy to let, such as city properties, which could be let all year round, to properties that require good weather and luxuries, such as sea views and/or a swimming pool, or ease of access to attractions.

If you have a letting agent, visit your property regularly to make sure the property is being let, and that repairs and maintenance are being carried out. Use these visits to check out the competition too, and see whether your property is still good value for money or whether you can increase your rent. Find out how long it may take to sell your property and how much it would cost. Properties abroad are typically more expensive to buy/sell than in the UK and can take several years to sell.

Remember to take out specialist buildings and contents insurance on your holiday home, which should include public liability cover in case of injury or damage. For the pros and cons of holiday lets, see below.

The pros and cons of holiday lets

Pros	Cons
• Can help to subsidise your own holidays.	• Requires time and money investing in furnishings and repairs.
• Rental income is higher than an average buy to let on a weekly basis.	• Dealing with multiple tenants on a weekly basis.
• Providing the holiday let is in the UK and meets specific criteria (see opposite), you can offset any losses against your other income, not just the property income, reducing your overall tax bill. Always consult a tax expert before buying.	• Cost of other letting expenses, such as insurance, is high versus other buy-to-let options. • Property is usually some distance away, so you will require a trusted agent. • Seasonality can be shortened with changes in climate.

 For more information on holiday homes and tax, go to www.direct.gov.uk/en/MoneyTaxAndBenefits/Taxes/TaxOnPropertyAndRentalIncome/DG_4017930.

The pros and cons of social lets and niche letting schemes

Social let pros
- The rent is paid for by housing benefit and often from the local authority.
- In some cases, the local authority will handle the letting, rent collection and day-to-day running of the property.

Niche letting scheme pros
- They can deliver high returns.
- You can stay there for free for a fixed period, such as 28 days.
- Time and worry free as usually well serviced and maintained as part of an overall investment scheme.

Social let cons
- You are limited as to the type of property you can buy – mainly suitable for the elderly or families.
- Finance may be tricky as many lenders won't back social landlords.

Niche letting scheme cons
- Limited market to sell to, so demand can vary dramatically.
- Few options to gain finance to purchase and gear (see page 7) your investment monies.

Social let

A social let is a let to someone that is on benefits, or to a charitable organisation that lets rooms out to the disadvantaged. Typically, a property's value for a social let is lower than average, while rents remain similar, so they can be a good investment. For the pros and cons of a social let, see above.

Niche letting schemes

New products continually come on to the market to present new investment opportunities. These include serviced apartments and hotel rooms. After purchasing an apartment, ideally in a key international city that may have a shortage of hotel rooms, you receive a percentage of the annual income, typically 50 per cent, which is paid on a quarterly basis.

These properties are taken care of by a management company and all you have to do is buy the apartment and receive the proceeds. Sometimes they include free stays for yourself during the year, so buying in a city where you may need occasional accommodation can make them a good investment. For the pros and cons of niche letting schemes, also see above.

 For more information about demand, properties required and the likely rent you can expect for a social let, contact your local authority housing department.

Finance and insurance

When looking for finance for a buy to let, consider all the different packages available and what best meets your objectives. It is particularly important to seek specialist advice as buy-to-let mortgages are not regulated, which means that you won't have any redress if the product turns out to be unsuitable for you.

There are various ways of funding your buy-to-let investment:

- **Use any spare cash** you have for a deposit.
- **Remortgage** your own property if there is enough equity and you can afford the increased payments long term.
- **Let your own home** (let to buy), buy a smaller one to live in and invest spare cash in more properties.
- **Utilise bridging finance** (see page 94).
- **Sign up to an investment club** on a 'no money down' type of investment (see pages 92–4).

Your first port of call should be an IFA (see pages 27–8). Take with you detailed plans, including what you want to do and when, and whether your strategy is to buy off-plan, to buy one property and then remortgage when you have additional capital, or to borrow heavily and build your portfolio quickly.

An IFA will assess your current income and assets and will advise the best type of lending facility for you. Better still, he or she will search the market for different types of buy-to-let mortgages and insurance, and find ones best suited to your investment needs, including packages only available through IFAs and not accessible on the open market.

BUY-TO-LET MORTGAGE

The main lending criteria for a buy-to-let mortgage are:

- **The rent is 125–130 per cent of the monthly mortgage costs.** For example, if the mortgage costs £500 per month, rent will need to be a minimum of £625 to qualify. Some lenders will offer at 110 per cent.
- **The loan is 75–85 per cent of the purchase price.** For example, on a £150,000 property, the mortgage offer would be £112,500–£127,500, so your deposit would be the balance: £22,500–£37,500.
- **The property is let on a six-month assured shorthold tenancy agreement.** This allows possession to be regained by the landlord (or the lender if the landlord has defaulted on payment) after six months.

- **Standard property** (there are no structural defects) and they are not HMOs nor for social letting.

There may be a maximum loan to one landlord of £10 million, or no more than £1 million for a single property. The lending criteria are there for a reason: if the housing markets turn down, you may not be able to make the payments and consequently could lose your property.

Buy-to-let mortgage costs

You must compare all the costs of a buy-to-let mortgage throughout the investment period. Could you borrow

> **❝ Mortgage lending criteria are there as a safe guard in case of a downturn in housing markets. ❞**

more if needed, either for maintenance on an unsecured basis or to use your capital growth to remortgage and buy additional properties? What are the charges and are you allowed payment holidays if you have problems? The kind of costs you need to be aware of are:

- **Booking and administration fees can vary** from a few hundred pounds to over a thousand.
- **Mortgage valuation fee,** which pays for the lender to value the property. It is not the same as an independent survey, which you would commission.
- **Property re-inspection fee** if you want to remortgage the property or switch products.
- **Early repayment charges** if you sell the property before you had planned.
- **Repayment or interest only?** Mortgages for buy to let can be repayment, interest only or a combination. It's important to gain advice on this from your IFA and tax specialist.

If you start with an interest-only mortgage, also discuss with your advisers whether it is worth making additional monthly payments later to repay the loan amount. To do this, you should ensure you can afford the extra costs or start a savings scheme such as an ISA. If you can afford a repayment mortgage later on, you may be able to remortgage and get a better deal.

'NO MONEY DOWN'

This type of funding is typically offered by property investment clubs (see pages

---

Finding a buy-to-let mortgage

The internet is a good source of information on buy-to-let mortgages. For example, members of the Association of Residential Letting Agents (www.arla.co.uk) are available to talk to, and other sites, such as www.moneysupermarket.com, allow you to look at the different types of mortgages available. Compare mortgages by looking at the total cost of the period you expect to have the mortgage, including arrangement fees, and consider what would happen if you had to change your plans in the short term. To get the best deal – and therefore reduce the monthly outgoings – you will need as big a deposit as possible. The best mortgage rates available tend to be when you borrow 75 per cent or less of a property's value.

198–201), which negotiate discounts, typically with developers for newly built and off-plan properties. Discounts such as off the price of the property or the stamp duty paid, are typically 20 per cent. The example below shows how you can take out a mortgage on the full price of the property, which includes the deposit and fees. These deals can work, but only as long as the following things are accurate:

> **!** Beware of hidden charges. Typically, the fee is 2–4 per cent of a property's value (which would equate to £4,000–£8,000 in our example), and on top of this companies may insist that you use their legal and financial services, which can cost three or four times what you would normally pay. In addition, all sorts of other charges, such as a 'reservation fee' of £1,000 or more, may be applied. Once you add up all these costs you may find that your 'instant equity' has gone.

- **That the property can be sold for at least £200,000.** Many new builds in a slow growth market lose 10–20 per cent of their value in the first few years, potentially negating any discount given.
- **Rental values are high enough to cover your costs** – and there is not a 'flood' of properties for rent on the market at the same time.
- **Property prices continue to grow at least 5 per cent per year** to cover the costs of buying and selling a property.

How a 'no money down' deal works

Property value on the open market	£200,000
25% discount applied from club	£50,000
You purchase for	£150,000
Mortgage gained at 90% of £200,000	£180,000
Estimated cash back	£30,000
Costs of the buy to let	
Deposit required	£20,000
Mortgage set-up fee	£1,000
Mortgage valuation	£350
Survey fee	£400
Legal fees	£500
Total cost:	£22,250

Leaving you with a net cashback of £7,750 and potentially a further £20,000 'free equity' as long as the property can be sold for £200,000. However, you are also likely to incur a finder's fee, which may well be in excess of the net cashback.

Before accepting a 'no money down' deal, make sure that you:

- Visit the location of the property and check everything in the 'offer' pack from the company.
- Find out whether developers will sell directly to you, and how much for.
- Check the local property papers (or the tourist board for holiday lets) and see what similar properties are letting for.
- Visit local letting agents and check how long it takes to let properties, whether demand is increasing or decreasing and how much minimum rents will be.
- Request an independent survey from RICS to assess the property's value and rental potential.
- Include all the costs of running the buy-to-let property (such as insurance, maintenance, gas and electrical safety certificates, tenancy deposit scheme).
- Look closely at the additional costs that may be incurred by purchasing the property through a company's own legal and financial teams.

Always get an independent solicitor and IFA to check the deal offered prior to going ahead – even if you have to pay twice. Independent advice on these deals is essential.

BRIDGING FINANCE

A bridging loan is a short-term loan that lasts from a day to a few months. For example, if you want to buy a property but don't have time to remortgage your own in order to be able to afford the new purchase, then a bridging loan can be used until other long-term finance is in place.

This route – for which you need to accurately identify property prices and likely rental potential – is generally for experienced investors who are concentrating on a particular area that they know well. For bridging finance to work efficiently, you buy the property at a substantial discount using the bridging loan, refurbish it quickly, get it revalued in a matter of days and then remortgage at the new, higher, value.

The biggest advantage of bridging finance is that it is quick to obtain and applicable to properties that are difficult to fund, for example, those classed as 'uninhabitable'. One particular bonus for an investor is that turnaround for receiving the money can be as little as a week and so a property can be secured with a generous discount because you are able to finance it quickly.

It is possible, but risky, to obtain a 100 per cent bridging loan. For example, you could buy a property for £135,000, refurbish within a month and get a revaluation of £150,000 once the work is done. However, although this type of

" Bridging loans are for experienced investors working in a market they know well. "

finance is useful, it relies on a rising market and if prices fall, you can soon find yourself in trouble. It can also be very expensive to finance.

INSURANCE COVER

Insurance is often forgotten when assessing the annual running costs of a buy to let, but it is essential to protect your investment.

Buildings insurance: if you have a mortgage, you will need this insurance and some buy-to-let packages include cover for such emergencies as burst pipes and broken boilers.

Contents insurance: you will need this if you have a fully furnished property or any belongings of your own on the premises.

Property owner's liability insurance (public liability): you will need this in case a tenant or person visiting the property gets injured, dies or causes damage. Check that it covers anyone working at the property, such as a gardener. If not, you may require 'employer's liability' insurance as well.

Other insurances worth considering, usually referred to as 'landlord insurance', include loss of rent if the property has been damaged; cover for rent if you have any voids; and legal expense cover should you have any problem with your tenants and you need to take court action to evict them.

Cost of insurance

Insurance costs vary and you should shop around to get the best deals. Either buy for individual properties or as a package to cover your whole portfolio. You can include emergency cover for water, gas and electrics from general insurers or from appliance manufacturers or utility companies.

❝ Insurance costs are often overlooked when assessing buy-to-let costs, but it is essential to get cover and protect your investment. ❞

Websites to check out for insurance deals are www.designsonproperty.co.uk, www.landlordzone.co.uk/Insurance/insurance.htm and www.find.co.uk.

Buying the right property

The research needed before you invest in a buy to let may seem daunting. Check out each of the different types of investment outlined on pages 91–4 in your area to work out which one will help you achieve your financial investment objectives.

You need to ask yourself how involved you want to be in the buy to let. If you want to manage the property yourself, you should ideally be looking at property that you can get to easily rather than have to travel an hour or more each way. If you are a keen DIY person or have a good team of tradespeople, then you may want to look at buying a property that will require some work. If you are in full-time work, however, and only have the weekends spare, then opting for a property that is ready for tenants may be a better option.

FINDING A BUY-TO-LET INVESTMENT

Your priority is to find an area where you can afford to buy and where the properties will produce a rent that gives a good return. Don't assume that the better the area, the higher the rent as this may not be the case – do your research. Buy only in areas that suit the market you are aiming for (see pages 17–18).

If you can, it is worth 'watching the market' for a few months before you buy. You can start your research on the internet where it is worth looking for those sites that specialise in your market. Local newspapers, for example *Daltons Weekly* and *Loot*, should also have a specific day for rentals.

66 How involved do you want to be? 99

Jargon buster

Assured shorthold tenancy agreement The most common form of tenancy, at the end of which the landlord can repossess the property

 If you decide on buying a property that needs renovating, see the previous chapters on pages 55–82 for more details.

Properties that are already let

It may be worth starting off by buying a property that is already let. It may be easier to access finance as there is a proven income against the property, and it is especially useful if the legal agreements with the tenants are robust and they pay the rent on time.

To find such properties, talk to agents and look in local newspapers. The most popular place to find let properties is through local auction houses (see pages 67-9). However, you should make the following checks:

- Why is the landlord selling? Is it a tenant problem, or too many repairs on the property? Are there any issues with the neighbours?
- Have a full, independent survey on the property so you know the cost of any repairs required.
- Talk to the tenants and find out whether they are looking to stay or move on.
- Have the tenant/landlord contract checked thoroughly and ask for the current and the first tenancy agreement on the property. Make sure it's an assured shorthold tenancy agreement (see the Jargon buster, opposite).
- Ask for bills for running the property so that you can accurately assess the costs versus the revenue.

Letting agents

Once you have identified what you are looking for, visit local letting agents who specialise in your type of let and/or have the best market share in the area. Estate agents frequently have lettings departments, too, and may be able to find you a property to purchase complete with a prospective tenant.

The letting market moves fast and you need to have the latest information to hand. From agents' weekly lists find out what properties are available, which were let quickly and whether they let for the advertised price or less. Don't forget that some properties have already been let before they are advertised, particularly where demand is high.

Contact agents to find out what is in short supply and what they may be having difficulty in letting. Ask what might be coming on to the market that will affect future demand (such as new builds) and therefore rental prices.

 Websites to visit for research include www.rightmove.co.uk, www.findaproperty.com, www.belvoirlettings.com/ and www.leaders.co.uk/. *Daltons Weekly* website is www.daltons.co.uk and for *Loot*, go to www.loot.com.

Landlord groups

Ask for help and information from local landlord groups and associations (see below), particularly if you have a specific target group in mind. Companies, colleges and universities or local councils may have information on who is looking for what and how you might help.

> 66 View thirty to fifty properties a month and compare the income and capital growth figures on five to ten of these. 99

COMPARING DIFFERENT INVESTMENTS

You must look at the details of maybe a hundred properties a month, narrowing those to thirty to fifty properties to view and then comparing the figures of five to ten of those in detail to see what will give the best annual income and capital growth. Always check everything carefully and visit the area/site/property in person. The chart on pages 100–1 is an example of what you need to consider. There are companies that have software you can use to help assess all the costs and, indeed, they help you calculate your income, profit and tax. For example, go to www.property-tax-portal. co.uk and www.landlordzone.co.uk. However, if you are starting out, it is still a good idea to consult a property tax expert from the start and only look to use these systems once you have gained more experience.

Importance of the survey

Make sure you have an independent survey done on each property to find out what costs you might incur both now and over the time you own the property. A new roof can cost thousands of pounds and remember that flat roofs need replacing on a regular basis. Even if these repairs are not due in the next five years, try to get the cost off the asking price. Costs vary from £300 to £500 for a homebuyer survey and £500 to £1,000 or more for a full structural survey. Do not rely on the mortgage valuation survey as this may not be extensive. An independent surveyor will usually take more time and trouble assessing the property and will be more reliable as guidance to its true state of repair.

Make sure you get any work done that is highlighted in your survey. Some jobs may not always seem important at

---

 The key landlord groups are the National Federation of Residential Landlords (www.nfrl.co.uk/), the National Landlords Association (www.landlords.org.uk/) and the Residential Landlords Association (www.rla.org.uk/).

> ! As part of the surveying process, get a gas and electric safety check so that you can negotiate any repairs and ensure the property is ready to let the day you complete.

the time, but spending a few hundred pounds now could save a great deal more in the future.

LEGAL CHECKS

Before purchasing a buy to let make sure you can legally let the property to someone else, particularly if it is a leasehold flat where some agreements prevent subletting. The kind of questions you need to ask your solicitor are:

- What are the rights of way for the property? If it is a garden flat, can anyone else use it? Are any driveways that are shared?
- Are there any restrictions on use or change of use on a building? Is there anything that would prevent me from changing a house to two flats or a series of 'bedsits'?
- Are there any covenants on the property (see page 156), particularly if I intend to build on its large garden?

- Where do the property boundaries start and finish? Check out paths and drives and who owns fences – left, right and back.
- On a leasehold property, can I or a tenant sublet rooms?
- Are there any restrictions when selling; for example, not being able to put up a 'for sale' board? In the UK there are rules on how big the sign can be, so check first if it is legally allowed and if there are any restrictions on size/where you display the sign.

Check the ground rent and service charges for last year and this year and the likely rent for next year. See if there is any work that would require upfront payment or affect any tenants (such as replacing windows).

❝ There are a number of things to check before purchasing a buy to let, such as shared access, change of use and any covenants on the property. ❞

 Help to calculate buy-to-let costs can be found on www.paragon-mortgages.co.uk and www.ucbhomeloans.co.uk.

Buy-to-let example costing sheet

Make your costings for each property as accurate as possible. Don't guess the figures as even a miscalculation by £50–£100 a month could make the difference between you making a profit, breaking even or losing money. You need to include all the following costs plus any extras and then compare these for each property. Add as many columns as you have properties on your shortlist.

		Example (£)	Property 1	Property 2
Property value	A	150,000		
Purchase costs				
Deposit		30,000		
Legal costs		1,000		
Stamp duty		1,500		
Mortgage costs		1,000		
Survey fees		300		
Sub-total		**33,800**		
Preparing for rent				
Gas/electric safety certificate		300		
Renovation/repair		2,000		
Sub-total		**2,300**		
Costs until rented				
Mortgage		1,950		
Council tax		375		
Utilities (water, gas, electric)		150		
Service/ground rent charges		–		
Sub-total		**2,475**		
Sub-total of costs – deposit	B	**8,575**		
Total sum invested	C	**38,575**		
Ongoing annual running costs [1]				
Mortgage		7,800		
Agent fees		2,160		
Water bill		300		
Gas/electric safety certificate		300		
Maintenance		500		
Landlord insurance (also includes buildings/contents insurance)			300	
Voids (allow 1 month per year)		1,000		
Sub-total		**12,360**		

"Don't guess: a miscalculation of £100 a month could take you out of profit."

	Example (£)	Property 1	Property 2
Estimated rental income			
Agent 1	14,400		
Agent 2	15,000		
Agent 3	15,000		
Average of all three agents	14,800		
Annual rental income – running costs	**2,440**		
Investment return	**D**		
Estimated property value 2 years	162,318		
Estimated property value 5 years	177,352		
Estimated property value 10 years	201,415		
Estimated cost of sale	**E [2]**		
After 2 years	3,500		
After 5 years	3,800		
After 10 years	4,200		
Estimated capital return	**(D–A–B–E / C)**		
After 2 years	less than 1%		
After 5 years	39%		
After 10 years	100%		

[1] Ongoing costs include replacement carpets/curtains and updating kitchens and bathrooms. There are also annual gas and electrical safety checks, maintenance such as decorating and the costs of preparing and keeping the property ready for rent

[2] The estimated cost of sale includes estate agent fees, HIPs fees, legal fees and removal fees

When you have narrowed your choice to one or two properties, add the letting costs, which include finding a tenant, contracts, letting agent fees and inventory costs.

To download your own copy, vsit www.designonproperty.co.uk.

"Remember ongoing costs such as replacing kitchens, bathrooms, carpets and curtains."

Refurbishing a buy to let

When refurbishing a buy-to-let property, consider the market you are aiming to let to. You will then know if you should stick to the basics or whether you should aim for a standard or premium finish. Your budget must reflect your intentions.

If you can, it is a good idea to see what your competitors are doing by way of refurbishing their properties. Whoever you plan to let to, provide fixtures and fittings to that particular standard. Bear in mind, though, that it is rarely the case that the more you spend on these items the more rent you will receive. Your rental property is almost always a temporary home for the people who will occupy it and what they will care most about is the style of living that it represents. This will mean that while something like broadband is required, a plasma screen television in every room is not necessary and will not add to the income you receive.

Many first-time investors opt to do most of the work themselves but this may not be the best course of action as being inexperienced may lead to you running over budget and/or over schedule. You need to get a tenant in as quickly as possible to make the best of your investment.

PREPARING THE PROPERTY FOR RENT

Landlords have a legal duty to make sure that properties are safe for their tenants. There are many legal requirements that must be dealt with before letting out your property and these include not only the obvious ones, such as the safety of appliances (particularly in relation to electricity and gas), but also issues that may not immediately come to mind, such as the Data Protection Act, which you might need to sign up to before collecting information about tenants.

Gas

The safe supply, running and maintenance of any equipment that involves a gas supply is vital, and without an annual check (you must keep a record and issue it to the tenant within 28 days) by a CORGI registered tradesperson you cannot legally rent out your property. As a backup, you may wish to install carbon monoxide detectors at the property.

 For more information on deciding to do-it-yourself or get-someone-in, see page 76.

Electricity

Any electrical equipment supplied, as well as the electrical system itself, must be safe to use, and this is a legal obligation. It is also a good idea to check electrical equipment, such as kettles, immersion heaters and washing machines, at the beginning of the tenancy and then on an annual basis. Because of strict safety legislation on appliances installed by landlords try, if possible, to get tenants to supply their own appliances and suggest hiring if they don't own the equipment they need. If you have to supply them, leave clear instructions on how to operate them safely.

Since 2005, there is a legal requirement to use a qualified electrician to carry out major electrical work. Look for someone who is a member of the National Inspection Council for Electrical Installation (NICEIC) to do all your electrical work (see page 213).

Fire safety

All domestic upholstered furniture, both new and second-hand (unless made before 1950), must meet the fire resistance jrequirements set out in the Furniture and Furnishings (Fire Safety) Regulations, 1988. This applies to furniture provided to new tenants and replacement furniture provided to existing tenants. The furniture will be labelled with its status under the fire safety rules and the furniture it isn't labelled, it cannot be used.

Smoke alarms

Mains-operated smoke alarms that are interconnected (if one goes off, they all go off) have to be fitted on each level of a property if built after June 1992. If your property is older, you should still fit battery-operated alarms, also on each floor as recommended by the fire service, and located in the most effective places. To ensure the efficacy of these alarms, fit a new battery in each alarm each time a new tenant moves in. Ask them to keep an eye on the alarms and let you know if there are any problems.

Safety websites

Association of Residential Letting Agents: www.arla.co.uk (supplies a leaflet about safety for landlords)

Carbon Monoxide awareness: www.carbonmonoxidekills.com

CORGI: www.trustcorgi.com (the national watchdog for gas safety in the UK)

Fire safety advice: www.firekills.gov.uk and www.shelter.org.uk

National Inspection Council for Electrical Installation: www.niceic.org.uk (the electrical contracting industry's independent voluntary body for electrical installation matters)

Information about fire safety regulations can be downloaded from www.dti.gov.uk – 'A guide to furniture and furnishings (fire safety) regulations'. See also the *Which? Essential Guide to Renting and Letting* for advice on how to decorate your property.

Managing the property

When your property is ready to let, the first thing to consider is whether you want to manage the let yourself or employ an agent to do it for you. You must also be aware of your legal responsibilities.

USING AN AGENT

There are enormous advantages in using a letting agent, particularly if you are working full time. But this is not a regulated industry and if you don't choose your letting agent carefully, there is potential for bad practices to affect you. It is especially important that you carefully check any legal contracts they provide.

« The letting agent industry is not regulated, so choose carefully. »

Choosing a letting agent

You want a professionally qualified agent who can find you good tenants, and quickly. They should also know your target market well so they can accurately advise on the likely rent and how long it will take to let out so you can plan accordingly. They should be a member of a relevant association (see box, opposite); this is particularly important should you have a dispute with your agent as the association will have a complaints procedure.

The pros and cons of self-managing

Pros	Cons
• Saving money on letting agent's fees.	• Your time finding, checking and organising tenants.
• Learning the business – albeit the hard way!	• Location if you are more than an hour from the let.
• Making contacts, such as tradespeople.	• The letting agent will already have tradespeople and tenants arranged.
• Learning new skills, such as emergency plumbing.	• Lack of experience – let a professional teach you first.

 For further information on renting and letting, see the *Which? Essential Guide* to *Renting and Letting*.

Letting agent associations

Only work with agents who are members of one or more of these associations:

Association of Residential Letting Agents (ARLA): www.arla.co.uk
National Approved Letting Scheme (NALS): www.nalscheme.co.uk
National Association of Estate Agents (NAEA): www.naea.co.uk
Royal Institution of Chartered Surveyors (RICS): www.rics.org
UK Association of Letting Agents (UKAL): www.ukala.org.uk

A good agent will have separate departments dealing with letting and managing property and their details should always be up to date. Some agents also run seminars or networking evenings where you can meet other landlords who have been working with that particular agent.

A further option is to let through specific accommodation agencies, such as for students, nurses and the police and fire service. University accommodation departments will vet landlords and will act as mediators in any disputes. They can advertise your property free of charge and if you want to, you can still ask a letting agency to manage the tenancy for you.

Letting agent costs

The costs of an agent will vary from area to area, partly depending on how competitive the local market is. There are three services that a letting agent will offer you:

- **Finding a tenant(s),** which costs approximately 10 per cent of the annual rent.

- **Collecting the rent,** which costs around 12 per cent.
- **Fully manage** (the main contact for the tenant and organise inventories or fixing problems), when the charges are 15–17 per cent.

In addition, you may get inflated prices and extra fees added if an agent arranges for repairs and maintenance to be done to your property. Lettings agents may also charge:

- For advertising costs.
- A reservation fee.
- For a tenant's reference.
- An administration fee at the start of the tenancy.
- A fee for carrying out an inventory.
- A renewal fee every time a tenant renews their contract.

Other items to check with your letting agent are:

- What the agent will be dealing with, including repairs and arrears.
- Whether there are any fees on top of the rental commission.

105

- Whether there are charges when there are no tenants. This is only acceptable for a full management contract as the agent continues to be responsible for maintenance, but the fees should be reduced during a void.
- The length of notice to cancel (typically 1–3 months).
- Whether there is an 'estate agency' fee if you put the house on the market and then the tenant buys it. This is typically 1.5 per cent of the sale price and is payable whether or not the lettings agent is also acting as the sales agent.

It is important that you get an agent to make a separate list of all their costs as these may be 'hidden' in a very long contract. You must carefully read and understand the small print, and although not your responsibility, this applies to the tenant as well. Check the paperwork with a solicitor as he or she will be able to highlight anything unusual or restrictive in the agreement.

ESSENTIAL TENANT CHECKS

It is vital that you undertake formal checks on the property and payment schedule – without them your investment may soon become a financial burden. Do not accept reassurances from a letting agent. As the landlord, you should see all documentation and carry out the following checks:

- **Identity check:** see the tenant's passport or other official proof of identity, such as a driving licence. Make a copy or note any details you may need if there is a problem.
- **Credit check:** shows any bad credit record, including county court judgements (CCJs), against them, provided the person in question hasn't falsified details. If there is no record (for example, someone from abroad), ask for a guarantor and check them out instead.
- **Financial and/or character reference:** should include a reference from the tenants' current employer(s) – and a call to check it is valid.

MANAGING THE TENANCY

As a landlord investing in property for a financial return, you will always need to look at the cost of running the property versus the income. Good landlords may never have to pay to get a new tenant – if you do a good job, tenants may well recommend you to other people. You do have a responsibility to the tenant to ensure that:

- **There is someone available** (you or your agent) 24/7 in case of problems. It is in everyone's interest to know immediately, particularly if there are disasters, such as a fire or floods.
- **Any repairs are fixed promptly** – your assets as well as your tenants need looking after.
- **You give 24-hours' notice** if you need to go round and knock, don't use your key.
- **Annual checks,** such as on a gas boiler, are carried out.

- You keep note of any communication with the tenants in case there are subsequent problems.
- Monthly rent arrives on time. If not, act quickly and, if necessary, instruct a specialist solicitor to gain repossession.

YOUR LEGAL RESPONSIBILITIES

As a landlord you have a legal responsibility to ensure that the house is safe for tenants and that you respect their rights. Make sure that tenants understand their responsibilities from the start. These rights and responsibilities are laid out in the form of a 'contract', which for most mortgaged buy-to-let properties will be an assured shorthold tenancy agreement.

Assured shorthold tenancy agreement

This is a form of tenancy that ensures the landlord has a right to repossess the property at the end of the term specified in the tenancy agreement, which can be for any length of time. To be eligible for this form of legal agreement, the tenant must have exclusive possession to at least one part of the house, such as a bedroom. Most assured shorthold tenancy agreement contracts will include:

- Names, addresses and contact details of the tenant, landlord and letting agent.

Deposits paid after October 2006

Recognising the conflict surrounding deposits, the Government introduced new legislation affecting any deposit paid after October 2006. The Housing Act 2004 makes it a requirement that any landlord taking a deposit must safeguard it with a tenancy deposit scheme (TDS), under which the deposit must be returned (after any deductions) within ten days of agreement being reached on its amount.

There are two types of TDS: custodial, where the money is held by the scheme itself; or where the landlord or agent keeps the deposit, which is insured in case of a dispute. Both types are supported by the alternative dispute resolution (ADR) service, although it is the landlord (never the tenant) who decides if this is to be used. Whichever type of TDS is used, the deposit is put into an interest-paying account and is only released when both parties agree to any deductions.

The landlord must inform the tenant of how the deposit is to be protected within 14 days. Failure to do this means the landlord cannot service a Section 21 possession notice (where at least two months' notice is given by the landlord to resume possession), and will be penalised with a fine of three times the deposit.

- Details of the property.
- A list of the rights of both the tenant and landlord.
- Dates that the tenancy starts and finishes.

For more information on tenancy deposit protection, go to: www.direct.gov.uk. To run a credit check, for which you will have to pay a small fee, go to www.experian.co.uk, www.equifax.co.uk or www.callcredit.co.uk.

- **How much the rent is,** when and how it will be paid and when the rent will be reviewed. Include details of any interest charges on rent that hasn't been paid.
- **How much the deposit is** (usually a month's rent), when it will be returned, any money that will be held back and what will happen if there is a dispute.
- **What costs the tenant and landlord** are individually liable for.
- **How, by whom and when** repairs and re-decoration will take place and who is responsible for the garden.
- **What alterations** the tenant can and can't do.
- **Whether the tenant** can sublet any of the property.
- **Break clause** to bring the tenancy to an end – by the tenant or landlord.
- **Forfeiture,** which allows you as the landlord the ability to end the contract before the termination date, should the

tenant fail to comply with agreed obligations, such as paying the rent.
- **Whether or not children and pets** are permitted.
- **Renewal of the tenancy agreement.**

If you agree to be paid weekly, by law, you must provide the tenant with a rent book and fill this in every week when the money is sent or collected.

Proceeding towards repossession

The occasional bad tenant is almost unavoidable. You must act quickly if your tenant stops paying the rent, but act within the terms of the tenancy agreement. If the problems continue, consult a solicitor. The steps to take towards repossession are:

1 Serve notice on the tenant. Depending on the problem and the contract, this could be for immediate repossession or giving notice of two weeks or more. Ensure the correct forms are served (as prescribed by the court) or you will have to serve them again.
2 If the tenant fails to respond, the court sets a date for a hearing; up to two months.
3 Make sure that you have done everything correctly. If you don't, the judge may rule in favour of the tenant.
4 If all goes well, you will be granted a possession order, but this may take another six weeks for the court to serve.
5 If the tenant fails to leave, you will have to ask the court bailiff to enforce the order.

Selling a buy to let

There are various ways of cashing in your investment. Before you put it on the market see whether you can find some similar buy-to-let properties and try to establish how they sold, how long it took and which types got the best price.

Your tax adviser will also be able to help with advice, including the best time to sell, how to make sure you take advantage of the whole family's tax allowances, and other ways of minimising the tax bill. For example, if the property was or can be your main residence at some time this will greatly help your position regarding tax liabilities. Sometimes these plans need to be made months or years in advance and you need to be aware of that.

When you are ready to take action, approach suitable companies and organisations to discuss your options and the costs involved.

❝ There are good and bad times to sell to minimise the tax bill: ask your accountant for advice. ❞

WAYS TO SELL YOUR BUY TO LET

One hassle-free way to sell the property is to the tenants, if they can afford it of course, so why not ask them first? If they say 'no', here are the other options that you can take.

Selling with a resident tenant

Selling with a resident tenant will limit your market, but you may still get a good price and a quick sale to a cash buy-to-let investor. Selling such a property would normally be done at auction or through specialist buy-to-let property sale websites (see below).

To track what has sold and how much for in your area, sign up to the Essential Information Group's website (see below) or visit your local auction house. To be useful, you should try to establish what similar lots have sold for in the last three to six months.

 For more information on tax on your property, see the *Which? Essential Guide The Tax Handbook 2008/9*. Investment websites include www.belvoirlettings.co.uk and www.buytolet4sale.com and www.eigroup.co.uk.

Case Study | Chris and Rosemary

Chris and Rosemary decided to invest in two properties to help towards the cost of paying for their children's education later on and potentially giving the children some additional monies to help them to pay for a property of their own. Having had a look around at properties locally they found it quite difficult and too time-consuming, so turned to a property investment club to get them two buy-to-let deals.

They bought one home (Home A) for £200,000 with a deposit of £30,000 and rented it out for one year. The value increased a year later to £230,000 so they remortgaged and borrowed against this one to invest in another (Home B) for £150,000 with a deposit of £30,000. After 11 years they sold both properties for £300,000 and £200,000 respectively.

Their initial investment costs were increased by the fact that they had to pay a 2.5 per cent finder's fee, which increased the buying costs by £8,500. The total costs of buying and selling each property was:

Home A: £15,803 + deposit = £45,803
Home B: £12,278 + deposit = £42,278

The capital gains made on each property were:

Home A: £84,197
Home B: £37,722

From an income perspective, the income and costs were:

Property A (£200,000)

	Year 1	Years 2–6	Years 7–11
Income	£15,000	£16,200	£18,000
Mortgage	£12,744	£13,200	£15,000
Water bill	£400	£400	£400
Maintenance	£1,500	£750	£1,250
Gas/electric checks	£250	£325	£375
Landlord insurance	£300	£350	£400
Voids	None	£1,350	£3,000
Gross income	–£194	–£175	–£2,425
Gross income over period	–£194	–£875	–£12,125
Gross income over 11 years –£13,194			

Property B (£150,000)

	Year 1-2	Years 3-5	Years 6-10
Income	£12,000	£13,800	£14,400
Mortgage	£8,904	£10,200	£9,000
Water bill	£250	£300	£400
Maintenance	£500	£400	£700
Gas/electric checks	£250	£325	£375
Landlord insurance	£250	£300	£350
Voids	None	£1,150	None
Gross income each year	£1,846	£1,125	£3,575
Gross income over period	£3,692	£3,375	£17,875

Gross income over ten years £24,942

Home A achieved a total gross return of 155 per cent, and over 11 years this equated to 14 per cent per annum, which even though they had poor returns from an income perspective, a good gain in capital made it a successful return.

Home B gave a good rental income throughout the period, giving just over 5.9 per cent return per annum, but didn't gain as much on a capital basis, giving just over 8.9 per cent return.

The tax implications with this case are complex as Chris and Rosemary are looking at investment for a capital gain, rather than income. As such, they may not be treated purely as a property investor (see page 202) and they should have sought specialist tax advice.

Selling through an estate agent

If priced correctly, it should take six to ten weeks for an estate agent to get an offer on your property and then a further three to four months to complete the sale. If you have a paying tenant, you can still market the property with his or her agreement, and your tenant can then remain in the property until the sale is completed.

Choosing an estate agent is covered in the chapter Renovating for profit – see pages 78–9.

Selling privately

You can try to sell the property yourself on private websites (see below). The upside of selling yourself is that you can save on agents' fees, the downside is that you have to manage the sale from offer to completion, including uploading all the information and photographs, organising viewings and attending them and checking your potential buyer's financial status. It can be tiring and time-consuming, so consider all your options and what is important to you. An agent may be more expensive but using one could be worthwhile for your peace of mind.

Sitting tenants

Sitting tenants are tenants that are already in situ when you buy a property and they can be a problem – it may not always be in their best interests to move out and so they may not present the property at its best and/or may restrict access. To help, you could offer the tenant a reduced rent or money on completion of the sale in return for their co-operation, but don't pay upfront or they may not deliver!

SELLING IN AN EMERGENCY

Even in an emergency, you will want to maximise your sale price. First ask your local auction house and estate agent if they can quote a price for a 'forced sale' of two to four weeks. Don't be greedy – price it in the bottom 10 per cent of similar properties and prepare to sell for 10 per cent below its value rather than risk repossession.

If you are a member of a landlord association, they may be able to find you a buyer. Alternatively, there are companies that specialise in these quick purchases – but beware! – some are less scrupulous than others. Look for offers of 85–90 per cent of the true market value. Get a valuation; compare it with your two to four week forced sale price; look at sale price data and, most importantly, pay for your own independent survey and valuation to make sure that someone isn't taking advantage of your situation. Finally, get your own, independent solicitor to check out all the terms and conditions associated with buying the property.

> **❝There are companies that specialise in quick purchases, but be careful who you deal with as some are less scrupulous than others.❞**

Suitable websites for selling a property privately are www.houseweb.co.uk and www.propertybroker.co.uk.

Building for profit

Building for profit is where you find a piece of land or a mix of building(s) and land and build one or more properties. It is one of the best ways to earn money from property investment – but it also brings with it high risk and a lot of hard work while the properties are being built.

Build your investment

Investing your hard-earned cash in a building project will either be something that really excites you or something that you think is way beyond your comfort zone.

SHOULD I BUILD?

Great returns don't come easily. To build for profit is a risky business – see the pros and cons, below. You can spend lots of money upfront to assess the project and then end up not securing the land or the permission you need. You also have to involve lots more people, including the local council and building control. Then there are rules and regulations you have to adhere to, which means you have less control of the outcome than you would with other forms of property investment. To help yourself:

- **Secure a reliable source of lending.** You will need to have a loan facility that is flexible and understands the ups and downs of property investment. You don't want someone pulling their funds or refusing credit when you really need it.
- **Buy at the right price.** Over pay for land or on building the project and you will lose money from the start.

The pros and cons of building for profit

Pros	Cons
• Often easier to build from scratch than to renovate, especially if you have outline or detailed planning and services to the site.	• It is very difficult to find the right plot at the right price as you compete with those wanting to make a profit as well as self-builders who are less worried about profit margins.
• Good returns on initial investment, around 30 per cent or more.	• Securing accurate quotes for a job that is not yet confirmed prior to making an offer on a plot is not easy.
• Can be quick to build if you buy in labour and materials, such as a timber-framed kit, which can be built in a matter of months.	• Timescales of the build rely on many third parties, such as the finance company releasing funds and builders sticking to schedules.

- Check that you have or can secure planning permission to carry out the work you want. Even the major builders only buy land subject to gaining planning permission and for some projects this can take years. They have the resources to do it and have existing land banks and projects that can generate the money required in the meantime, but it's unlikely that you will.

- Ensure you can achieve a fast turnaround on the project. To make the project work as smoothly as possible:
  - Buy land that already has outline or detailed planning permission (OPP or DPP) or purchase a property with land that you can renovate and sell on or pull down and make way for the new property.
  - Check there is the required vehicle access for builders' equipment.

Potential return when building for profit

Below is an example of the type of return that could be made on your initial investment with a successful project.

Purchase price		Funded by	
Land price	£100,000	Mortgage	£211,500
Build costs	£135,000	Deposit	£23,500
Total purchase price	**£235,000**	**Total**	**£235,000**

Additional costs			
Research	£6,000		
Mortgage payments (during project)	£12,000		
Buying and selling	£8,500		
Total additional costs	**£26,500**		

Profit			
Sale price	£305,500		
Less purchase price	£235,000		
Less additional costs	£26,500		
Total profit	**£44,000**		

Total investment = deposit of £23,500 plus additional costs of £26,500 = £50,000.

Return on investment = profit divided by total investment.

Therefore, the return on investment = £44,000 / £50,000 = 88%.

Project management skills

You need to:

- Understand building schedules, what needs to be done first and last.
- Liaise with planning and building departments.
- Order the right materials at the right time and ensure they are on-site when needed.
- Manage lots of people to ensure they do the job they said they would, when and at the price you've agreed to pay.
- Problem solve on a daily basis.

If you haven't got the right skills to do this, it is better to employ a professional as project management can make the difference between making a lot of money or losing it.

the budget and timescales and try to save time and money elsewhere on the project, without of course devaluing the end result.

- Hand over the project to a professional to manage (see page 126), or ensure that you have the time and skills to manage the project yourself. Remember this isn't an easy task (see left). Project management of a build is a complex skill that people train for years to do.

❝ Keep a tight rein on your budget – check progress daily to ensure costs are accurate. ❞

- Check there is an existing supply or easy access to services such as electricity and telecoms and gas/oil/ other forms of energy.
- Check there are no legal reasons such as restrictive covenants, which mean that you can't build, have to seek other people's permission or pay some of your profits to someone else.
- Keep a tight rein on your budget. It's very easy when spending a lot of money and working within a timescale of a year or more to build, to overspend or incur problems that cause costly delays. Every day check what needs to be done, whether it's done and if the costs were accurate. If there are any delays or overspends, then you need to review

! If you do find a property with planning, you may nevertheless wish to change the plans to create a project that maximises your investment. This could cause delays through negotiating and re-submitting plans to the local authority, and if they don't accept your revised versions, then you may have wasted your time and money buying the plot in the first place.

Finance and insurance

Organising funding for your project depends on the type of property you are building: commercial or residential, single dwelling or multiple properties. It is vital that you are clear about your objectives and seek the right finance company.

FINANCIAL CONSIDERATIONS

Finance for building projects is similar to renovation (see pages 60–2), but there are some subtle differences. When securing the finance that you need to build for profit you may:

- Be buying a commercial property and adding residential units.
- Be converting a commercial property to residential units.
- Need to borrow substantial sums of money for a large building project.

You need to secure funding that helps you buy the land and material and labour costs until you sell the property. It is vital that your mortgage or loan will:

- Give you money upfront for each stage of the development.

> ❝Before you approach commercial finance experts, know exactly what you want. ❞

- Be able to reassess your requirements during the build and lend more money if it is required.
- Loan monies beyond the limit of the monies you have already, such as against the equity in your own home.

It is critical that you understand the different ways of securing commercial finance from experts that are used to building-for-profit projects (see below). There are various ways of securing finance for small developers, ranging from major banks to specialist financing companies. However, before you approach commercial finance experts,

Specialist development finance

If you decide to take on a major project that requires a lot of money, for example £1 million or more, you may well need to secure specialist development finance that allows you to borrow large sums of money (albeit at higher loan rates and costs). As you may not have the cash to pay the loan charges over the period of the project on a monthly basis, this can be negotiated to be paid at the end of the project when you have received all of the cash from the sale of the properties.

you will need to have planned your strategy and have examples of the project(s) that you are expecting to carry out. You should also gather together details of your current financial situation (if you have a property company, you will need a minimum of two years of audited accounts, profit and loss sheets and bank statements) and have CVs for you and any partners.

The typical lending perimeters on building for profit projects are:

- Around 65 to 75 per cent of the cost of purchasing the land and building costs. However, if you have a good track record, you may be able to get 100 per cent.
- Projects should offer approximately 25 per cent profit on the costs.
- The amount loaned ranges from £100,000 to £25 million.
- Lending interest of up to 2.5 per cent above bank base rate.
- A minimum lending term of one year.
- Interest only loans.

The loan will only be made on evidence of full planning consents and the relevant certificates from the local council. Payments are then made in stages and the cash released when key build stages are completed.

When financing building projects, most companies will look to finance via senior debt first, and then if you do not have enough money to pay for the rest of the project, the financiers will turn to mezzanine and/or equity finance, each of which is described to the right.

Senior (bank) debt finance

This is effectively a commercial loan and is money that is lent on a short-term basis of one or two years. You borrow the money you need and pay back interest over the period of the loan. Then, once you have finished the project, you pay back the money you have borrowed. This is the most cost-effective way to borrow, but the bank has first call on their money should the project get into difficulties, and if you don't make a profit, you will still need to pay off the full amount of the loan.

Mezzanine finance

This type of financing is used to fill the gap between the bank loan and senior debt finance and is charged at a fixed, but higher, rate of interest than the bank loan, typically around 2.5 per cent more. The plus point of this type of finance is that the amount you pay back is fixed, and it can be helpful in the early days of residential development when costs can be high. The downside is the additional cost of the finance over the bank loan.

Equity finance

This is a form of financing that attracts other investors (either companies or individuals) and works by the investors offering money for the project in return for a 'share' of the project's profits. This finance can be essential to get a project off the ground, but tends to be more expensive than other financing as you will have to give away a share of the profit you make. For example, if the amount of equity finance required is

£250,000, and this equates to 25 per cent of the project costs, then you may well have to give away 25 per cent of the profit you make.

One hundred per cent finance

If you are a property investor that has experience in developing property and especially in the house-building industry, it may be possible to have the whole project funded from start to finish with 100 per cent lending. Clearly this can be a risky option (for both the lender and you), and you would have to forgo a share of the profit you would make and/or a fee that is agreed upfront and paid at an agreed point. However, if you have the experience and knowledge, but money is holding you back, then this may be a viable option.

This type of financing is not regulated by the FSA so take care in choosing the company you gain financing from.

CHOOSING A FINANCE COMPANY

Ideally, the company should be:

- Experienced at financing projects, large and small.
- Experienced at working with first-time property developers.
- Able to analyse and assess your project to ensure you are maximising the profit.

- **Able to check and advise** on all of your financial projections.
- **Prepared to work with you** on a regular basis to check that the project is on track.
- **Able to give you help and advice** should the project run into problems.

The company should also have access to as many different financing companies as possible to help you get the best deal.

Some companies may belong to the National Association of Commercial Finance Brokers (NACFB) (see below). Although membership won't guarantee the best help, it does give you a third party to go to should you not be able to overcome any complaints. If a company is claiming to be a member, always check that membership is current.

Running over budget

However well you manage your money, it may be that the project does run over at various points and you need a quick injection of cash to keep things on schedule. It is wise to negotiate this with your financial backer at the start of the process and agree what you need to provide to show that you require the funds and under what terms you will borrow the additional monies.

 Some sources for property development finance include: www.ardentfinance.com, www.cala.co.uk, www.mortgagesforbusiness.co.uk and www.wolseysecurities.co.uk. The website for NACFB is www.nacfb.org. See also pages 27–8 for finding an IFA who can also source residential property finance.

ORGANISING INSURANCE

Insurance for building projects is not dissimilar to renovation projects (see pages 62–4). To be able to draw down the monies you have secured, the following insurances will probably need to be in place prior to anything happening on-site:

- **Public and employer's liability.** You will be employing companies and contractors to work on the site and will require cover for any staff you have, other company employees as well as subcontractors you directly employ.
- **On-site building materials and equipment.** The value of the materials you have on-site will be phenomenal so it is important to make sure that you have sufficient cover should the worst happen.
- **Buildings insurance.** You need this during the time that you are building the properties and for when they are completed.
- **Legal expenses.** This is to cover any problems you may have with the companies you are working with.

Structural warranties

In addition to the insurances listed above you will need to purchase a structural warranty, which is an insurance that protects the purchaser of the property for ten years. The warranty covers the purchaser as described to the right.

- **Bankruptcy.** If you can't finish the project because you run out of money, this insurance pays out for anyone who has already paid a 10 per cent deposit and bought 'off plan' or early in the build.
- **Defects.** If any defects are found with the property, the insurance will pay out to put the property right if you don't do so for any reason.
- **Structural insurance.** This is to protect the owner and property from structural problems such as issues with the foundations, drainage, chimneys and roof, walls and things like staircases and windows. It won't protect the purchaser from general wear or tear on a property.
- **Contaminated land.** Hopefully you will have solved this problem (see page 123) before you build, but if there are any issues that appear after the owners have moved in, the purchaser is then covered for the problem being put right.

Be aware that building warranty companies usually require you to use (and pay for) their own building inspectors to sign off every stage of the build. By law, you will have to have these inspections, but make sure you know exactly what the costs are prior to agreeing to use one of the warranty companies.

 There are three main companies that provide structural warranties. Their website addresses are: www.nhbc.co.uk/, www.premierguarantee.co.uk and www.zurich.co.uk/.

Where and what to build?

Finding and securing your ideal plot requires tenacity. You will then need plenty of creativity to decide how you can adapt the area for maximum profit.

FINDING A PLOT

There are lots of resources you can go to, including some residential estate agents, commercial agents and auctions (see pages 67–9). Also look online and contact local developers who sometimes sell part of the plots they own for others to develop.

It is also worth looking at the council's local plan to see what areas they have designated for potential development and then see if the owners of these areas are keen to sell and, if so, at what price.

Finally, drive around as much as possible. Look for derelict buildings in areas that already have properties on them, or where building is taking place and there is more 'space' that you could look at buying next to the current development or nearby.

Costs depend on what's on the site that needs to be taken down. However, the most important factor will be the location of the land and who else is competing with you to buy it.

WHAT TO BUILD

Deciding what to build on the land you have secured may be obvious to you – or you may have no idea. In some ways it may be better to have no idea, because then you would be in an ideal position to research from scratch what scenarios would give you the best profit. This is preferable to going with what you would like to build, which might not be the most profitable option.

In most property investment projects you make your money when you buy. This is also true when developing for profit. But the difference between making a profit and little or no return is the control you have over the build (see pages 125–9). Equally important is the speed at which you sell the properties. Don't forget that you will be paying interest on the loan from the time you start drawing it down, so you need to carefully consider the time it will take to sell. If it takes years rather than months, you could run out of profit very quickly. So if you think you know

 One good online facility for finding a plot of land is www.buildstore.co.uk; search for 'commercial plots'. For more information on gaining accurate quotes and budgeting, see pages 126-8.

what you want to build, make sure you check it with local experts before you go ahead and buy.

Talk to experts

Talk to the local planners, the council housing departments, building control and local estate/letting agents. Ask them what it is they think the area is desperate for now and in the next 12 months to two years. Find out the minimum price that you could sell the properties for – not the maximum as that can quickly become a misleading figure.

These discussions can be invaluable and save you a fortune as you should then be extremely clear on:

- **Areas where land can be developed** (see pages 134–9).
- **Your development's impact** on the local infrastructure.
- **The type of property that planners are looking for** – or specifically won't pass.
- **Any restrictions or conditions of development** that you need to consider.
- **Any latest building regulations,** or ones that will be in place in the next 12 months, that you need to adhere to.

Size of the development

Don't forget that property prices can turn up or down within months, so work out what would happen if you funded the project but had to sell at 10 per cent below the initial value you were hoping for. Then, if prices increase more than you expect, you gain additional profit from rising prices, rather than relying on price increases to make the return you need.

Evaluating the best return from a building project takes expertise, often specialist software and a lot of time. It is important to have help during this process from surveying practices, residential development experts that may end up financing your project and some estate agency and commercial agent firms.

It may be that one plot would give a better return with flats, others with as many terraced houses as permitted, whereas some sites fare better with a mix of flats, terraced and detached homes. Each will have different costs, building time and a different sale price and time to sell. As a result, the profit level will differ for each and you need to make sure you take on the project that maximises the return on your investment.

There may also be restrictions placed on you as to the number of properties you could build on one site. For example, the local planners may have certain properties that they want built and they will give you a guideline of the square footage that each property needs to have.

This is something that an experienced architect would be able to advise on, but you might as well get the information for free and start building a relationship with the planning office prior to looking for a plot to buy so you can easily assess them from the start.

Land with an existing property

Alternatively, you can look at buying land with a commercial or residential property already on the plot. On such sites, there are many ways that you turn a profit.

How many properties can you have per hectare?

This varies according to the type of property, such as flats, detached, semi-detached or terraced properties, and the number of rooms per property. The planning office will also take into consideration vehicle access and the area that you are developing.

For example, in high-density areas such as towns or cities you are more likely to be allowed more properties per hectare than you would be in lower-density areas. Another measure the planning office will consider is the 'plot ratio', which calculates the floor space of all the properties combined with the total size of the plot.

You can gain this information prior to even finding a plot by talking to, visiting or looking at your local council's planning guidelines.

For example, if you buy a block of single storey flats or one or two shops, there may be the opportunity to build on top of them. Or you may buy a large property and divide it into flats, or buy property with a lot of land (for example, a bungalow or corner plot), tear it down and build several properties in its place.

LAND ISSUES

Whatever your plans, it is important to know what land you can build on cost effectively and the problems that can occur, which could increase your costs and therefore reduce your profit margin:

- **Ensure you can build on the site.** As with property, land is designated for certain uses. These include greenbelt, agricultural/greenfield, woodland, grazing or equestrian, farmland and brownfield. The only ones that are likely to be eligible for planning in the short term are brownfield sites. These currently include land that already has planning permission for new builds, including large plots of land with one property on that can be restored or another where the property can be pulled down.

- **Be aware of what type of soil the land consists of** and what is lurking underneath. The types of soil that are ideal to build residential properties on are peaty, silty, sandy or loamy as they naturally drain well or you can ensure they are easy to build on and grow plants for gardens.

- **Other issues such as contamination.** If you are developing a site that already has property on it, you need to be aware of what environmental issues you may have to deal with. For example, old petrol stations or factories often have to have special treatment such as taking out any existing tanks, and sites previously used for landfill require a membrane to stop any gases coming up. Landfill doesn't just affect the land built on it, it can contaminate surrounding land for about 250 metres and beyond.

Land searches and surveys

To find out more about your proposed plot, get an environmental search done. It will tell you about flooding, contamination and issues such as previous development and potential subsidence caused by activities such as coal mining.

However, an environmental search is only based on postcode and you will need to have a land survey done by an expert from the Royal Institution of Chartered Surveyors (RICS) (see below). It is wise to choose a surveyor that is experienced in land and development and you will need to:

- **Give or discuss the plans** that you have to develop the land.
- **Show the drawings of the plot of land** to the surveyor and ensure that you are clear on the area that you are buying – and it matches the information given with title deeds.
- **Ask for any information about the land** that might increase your costs of development.
- **Visit the site** with the surveyor.

Once your surveyor has visited the site, he or she will do a report, which will:

- Give the value of the land.
- Include a topology survey explaining why the land is shaped as it is and what may be beneath the surface.

- Give clear boundary measurements.
- Indicate the viability for your development plans.
- Highlight any issues of flooding or other environmental checks that might be an issue or require further investigation.
- Include any issues to consider with regard to access, which may affect planning approval, or check existing plans that have been passed and whether you can make any changes, if required.

The report may also recommend you make further investigations, such as soil testing or further examination by an environmental surveyor. In some cases, the planners may even request that you do further surveys on the land that relate to the protection of endangered species and, indeed, trees that may have a conservation order on them.

These surveys can be very expensive, so make sure you understand the full extent of any further research and the costs prior to committing to purchasing the land/property.

Apart from assessing the land's value and its viability for residential development, surveyors do a lot more than when surveying a home. They are also experienced at negotiating to buy land with options, for example, only completing on a purchase if the land gains planning permission.

 To get a free view of the type of land, insert the postcode you are looking at on www.homecheck.co.uk. You can then order a proper review, which includes drainage searches. The website for RICS is www.rics.org.

Managing the project

Managing a major building project can rarely be done successfully on a part-time basis. It's really a full-time job for someone experienced at managing building work.

USING THE RIGHT PEOPLE

Even before you start your project, surround yourself with experts. Then, once you have decided on what you are going to do, your team is in place to successfully carry out the project with you – on time and to budget.

Planning specialist and architect

If you require any changes to plans that have already been passed you will need to hire a planning specialist and architect. A planning specialist has a detailed understanding of the local rules and regulations and should have contacts in the local planning office. The architect's job is to create the drawings for the planners to view and pass. They will detail the measurements and give the planners the information they require on how and what you are using to build it.

Ensure your architect is up to date with the latest building regulations or that the drawings are passed by a building control expert prior to sending them to the planning office. It can substantially delay your build if the planners pass your drawings but they are then rejected by the local building control officer.

Builder and subcontractors

Finding a good builder that can take on the job from start to finish, or putting together a series of contractors, can take over a year to do. So it's important to have someone in mind when you are looking for land. You need to be aware of their availability and have their input at the time when you are putting together the drawings and choosing materials to work with. They may otherwise raise issues after the plans have been approved. You will be working with the builder (or subcontractors) on a daily basis for months if not a year or more and it's a good idea to build a good working relationship prior to starting the project, while tension isn't too high.

If you are thinking of employing a series of subcontractors, see the tradespeople section on page 213). Bear in mind that you may also have to find a ground clearance company.

❝Finding the right builder for the job is crucial. Have someone in mind even when you are just looking for land. ❞

Who will manage the project?

If you find the thought of managing the project too much, there are three different ways that you can reduce the responsibility:

- Employ a full-time project manager. Your costs may increase, but a project manager has a network of contacts and knows where to get materials at a better price than you, or even your architect. Ensure that his or her costs can be off-set against the savings that can be made on your behalf.
- Your architect or builder may take on this role. Ensure they have the experience required and have references from happy customers – ones you have met and sites that you have seen. Agree on whether or not this service is a part of the contract.
- Work closely with your local builder's merchant. Many of these companies, such as Jewson or Build Centre, have local account managers who will help to cost out the materials and build schedules. Usually this is in return for the materials business, but if you get a good price, this service can save lots of time.

GAINING ACCURATE QUOTES AND BUDGETING

When you have a large budget on a project, it can be all too easy to overspend by as much as 20 per cent, which can wipe out your profit. That's why it is essential to list every cost upfront to ensure that you work from the right figures. You can also borrow exactly the right amount of money, at the right time (see the budget plan on page 73).

It's easy to worry only about the big costs, but it's actually the smaller costs that can really push you over budget. When you are spending £100,000 on land, £50,000 on materials and £60,000 on labour, it's easy not to add in other costs, such as landscaping, house showing and selling costs, but these can add a further £10 to £20,000 to your costs and need to be budgeted for. Every project cost will be different. If you are building properties, the build costs are likely to be broken down as follows:

- Land/project: 50 per cent
- Labour: 25 per cent
- Materials: 25 per cent

They can, however, vary substantially.

Buying costs

These vary depending on how you purchase the property. If you buy directly, there are unlikely to be any fees associated, but if you find the land/project through an internet site, these will cost around £100 to join.

If you buy through auction, you will need to consider paying a subscription cost for an internet website, which will be around £300 per year, then the fees for the auction catalogue of around £300. You will then incur the usual buying costs (see the table, below).

Ongoing costs

Once you have bought the land and/or property there are costs to pay even before you start to build. These may include: insurance; loan repayment; fencing and signage; on-site security; architect fees; planning and building regulations fees; Standard Assessment Procedure (SAP) rating certificate; tender costs; on-site services/utilities survey and site clearance.

Build costs

These are the most complicated part of building for profit and the hardest to get right. However, there is an enormous amount of help that you can get for costing out your build project – some of it for free from building material companies – and it's worth drawing on all the help you can as it's such an important part of the process.

Managing your cash flow

Building for profit is just like running any business. You have a list of things to do and people that you need to help you get the work done. However, the only difference with a building project is that until the project has got to a certain stage, money is just going out rather than coming in.

If you are working on a small project such as a building a single new home or converting another into flats, then the cash flow should be fairly straightforward. However, you need to maximise your money at all times. For example, there are many ways of keeping the money in your pocket, earning interest. You can do this by delaying drawing down a loan and paying the repayments:

- **Negotiate on payment of work.** If you employ an architect, you can agree to pay some of the fees upfront, part on a monthly basis and pay the balance once the plans have been passed by both the planning and building

Example buying costs

Item	Fee: small property	Fee: multi-site project
Legal fee	£500	£2,000+
Land registry fee	£150	£250+
Mortgage administration/booking fee	£500	£2,000+
Mortgage valuation	£500	£1,000+
Survey fee	£500	£2,000+

regulations office. You can also negotiate stage payments with your builder and subcontractors, withholding the last payment until the project is finished and all the work has been done to the satisfaction of yourself, building regulations and your insurance warranty company.

- **When purchasing materials,** it is always possible to negotiate favourable terms. For example, if you give merchants enough evidence that you can pay for goods on time, you may well be able to negotiate 30–60 days' credit.

There is nothing worse than running out of money and delaying the project or having too much money in the bank that you are paying interest on. So carefully track your monies on a daily, weekly and monthly basis. Check to see what you forecast and then what has actually happened. This way, if there is any overspend you can make cuts to bring the budget back into line. Equally, if there is an underspend, you can work out if you can delay drawing down your next loan and incurring higher than necessary loan repayment costs.

TIMINGS

As much as it's important to get the costings right for a project, getting your timings as accurate as possible is just as critical. When you are borrowing lots of money, running over by a month could eat into your profits.

The key timings to be aware of are listed opposite. Most can be run alongside each other, so for example, in the pre-offer stage, once you have drawings and materials from the architect, you can get building cost quotes when you ask the planning office to give you feedback on your drawings.

GUARANTEES AND CERTIFICATES REQUIRED

To sell your project legally you will need all the certificates and paperwork to show that everything has been done legally and to a required standard. At the start of the build, you will need:

- A copy of the planning approval document.
- One master copy of the approved plans and several copies of the latest plans.
- Copy of building regulations approval.
- List of the stages of build that you need to gain building regulations sign-off.
- List of the stages of sign-off for your new-build warranty insurance, which may be done in conjunction with the building regulations sign-off.

If you are developing more than one property, you can apply for two different types of building regulations: type approval and system approval.

 For more information about managing cash flow and stage payments and cost estimating systems, go to www.buildstore.co.uk, www.buildthedream.co.uk and www.hbxl.co.uk.

- **Type approval,** where a standard design of building types such as timber frame or brick and block is given a nationally recognised certificate. With this scheme you get a 'LABC (Local Authority Building Control) Approved' logo to help market the property.
- **System approval,** which provides a certificate that is given for properties being built with the same components and construction detail, albeit in a variety of different designs. This scheme is especially useful for non-traditional building systems, but you don't get an 'approved' logo for this type of sign-off.

Planning time: an example

Pre-offer	Length of time
Provisional architect drawings	2-4 weeks
Submit drawings to planning for provisional approval	2-4 weeks
Gain quotes for building costs	2-4 weeks
Post-offer	
Finalise drawings subject to recommended changes from planners/building regulations	2-4 weeks
Submit to planners for approval	8 weeks
Draw up a schedule of works	2 weeks
Confirm build costs	2-4 weeks
Appoint a builder	Varies
Building schedule	
Ground clearance	4 weeks
Foundations and drainage	2-4 weeks
Constructing walls/floors to first floor	4-8 weeks
Constructing walls to roof plate level	2-4 weeks
Roof construction	2-4 weeks
First fix electrics and plumbing	1-2 weeks
Plastering/wall finish	1-4 weeks
Second fix electrics/plumbing and heating	1-2 weeks
Landscaping	2-4 weeks
Decoration and finish	1-4 weeks

 For more information, go to the LABC website at www.labc.uk.com and search for 'A Quick Guide to Controlled and Exempt Building Work'. For more information on planning and building regulations approval, go to www.planningportal.gov.uk.

Selling the property

When major developers start to sell properties, there is rarely anything to see but a piece of ground, which has not even been cleared. However, they often have fancy plans of what the plot/space is going to look like, fabulous websites and brochures to give away and lots of experienced sales staff to boost their sales before a block has been laid.

Just because you haven't the budgets that larger developers have, doesn't mean you can't employ most of their sales tactics. Even before you secure the land and project you can start marketing what you are going to do – either by talking to local agents or to locals who might be interested in buying a property that you build for them.

You can potentially sell the property off-plan from the day you secure the land and the planning permission. There are many ways you can market your plot and property:

- **Advertise your company** and telephone number on a board on the fencing (check you are within the planning rules).
- **Convert your architect's plans to drawings** for a board and/or brochure advertising.
- **Produce a website** providing information and the number of properties you are producing, when they will be completed and pictures of what they will look like.
- **Secure an agent** to produce the property details.

- **Ensure you gain a listing on an appropriate property portal** and advertising in the local property paper.

SELLING PRIVATELY OR THROUGH AN AGENT

You can sell your properties privately, or via an estate agent. The upside of selling yourself is that you will save money on estate agent's fees. The downside is that you may not have the time to do the selling or may make mistakes.

Choosing an agent

Choose your agent very carefully as making the wrong choice can cost you time – and therefore money. Ideally choose an agent that is used to dealing with smaller developers, but also one that is enthusiastic about your project and has buyers on their books looking for the kind of property you will be selling. Many have their own 'land and new homes' division, which can be an advantage.

The main issue that you need to be aware of is that an estate agency is only as good as its management and best sales negotiator. Employee turnover is extremely high in estate agency, so make sure that the people you sign up at the start are the same people that are going to sell your property.

Don't forget that estate agents are by nature negotiators. Time to you is money, so try to 'incentivise' them as much as possible if they sell near to, on or above the asking price. Even better would be if they were to sell off-plan and guarantee you a sale, as well as money upfront that can be used to pay off your loan early.

Accepting an offer

If you are selling off-plan and are nervous about meeting your loan payments, or think the project may be behind, consider accepting a lower offer to secure an early sale. You can only exchange, but that means you could take a 10 per cent deposit and so improve your cash flow. It also shows your financial backers that your property is in demand, which, if you need any further help or support, can be extremely useful.

Most developers will first ask someone to 'reserve' a plot at a set cost, up to £1,000. This means no one else can be sold that plot, normally for 28 days or until you have exchanged, whichever comes sooner.

Accepting an offer so early can sometimes put you in a difficult situation when you have someone that has reserved a property, but can't complete as they haven't sold their own property or their buyer has pulled out. In these circumstances, turn to help from outsourced part-exchange providers (see below), who will purchase your buyer's property so that, in turn, your purchaser can continue to buy yours.

Part-exchange providers

Part-exchange is a powerful marketing tool, as are other incentives such as offering to pay stamp duty or give a discount off the property or free carpets and curtains. The way it works is that you give a part-exchange company (see below) the details of the vendor and they will either visit or research the property and make an offer to buy it, which varies between 85 and 90 per cent of its value. They will buy most second-hand properties, but you are likely to have to make up the difference to a point. So if they offer to buy the property at £20,000 less than its market value, the buyer will no doubt expect you to drop the price of your property. However, there are no estate agent fees involved and you do at least get a guaranteed sale on a guaranteed day. In the main, part-exchange providers won't buy a property until a minimum of 12 weeks before the property is ready for the purchasers to move into.

For more information on choosing an estate agent, see pages 78-9. Websites for part-exchange companies include www.arcpropertygroup.co.uk, www.quickmoveproperties.co.uk and www.pxsproperties.com/.

Case Study Ahmed

Ahmed worked in the building trade as a surveyor and was keen to get on the property ladder, but knew that buying a ready built property versus buying the land and building from scratch would mean he could get more for his money and potentially sell on the property at a good enough profit to take another step on the property ladder in the future.

He put down a 5 per cent deposit to borrow a mortgage, which covered £60,000 for the land and £60,000 for labour and materials. His build costs included:

Labour	£30,000
Materials	£30,000
Warranty	£2,000
Insurance	£600

He managed to keep the costs coming in almost on budget, investing a further £2,600 on the warranty and insurance. To save money renting a property, he stayed on-site in a caravan for the duration of the build, which cost a further £1,600 to buy. As the property was being built, Ahmed had some interest in it and with local property prices rising during the build, he agreed to sell on completion for £165,000. The final income was therefore:

£165,000 gain from the property minus:
£120,000 mortgage loan
£10,570 in buying/selling and mortgage fees
£4,200 in additional costs.

This made his total gain: £30,230 and with an initial investment of £20,770 (deposit plus costs) gives an annualised return of 145 per cent.

However, as Ahmed has never lived in the property, he may well be subject to tax on the gains made and may well have been better off living in the property for a period of time, he would have been able to legitimately sell it and not incur any capital gains tax (see page 202). Tax and legal specialist advice should sort this out to maximise profit and minimise the tax bill.

Landing a good return

Buying land as an investment is something that has never been more popular, or potentially more lucrative. The availability of land is finite and so the pressure on existing land becomes increasingly acute. Acquiring the best quality land in the right location and at the right price requires considerable knowledge on your part and that of independent experts.

8

Investing in land

The returns on land investment are potentially extremely lucrative, but as with anything that requires a degree of speculation, cannot be guaranteed.

Remember, however, that land investment is likely to involve risking a lot of cash – your hard-earned cash – as the possibility of gearing your money by means of loans or mortgages is more difficult unless you are buying a farm with residential buildings. If you can secure lending, you are only likely to get a loan-to-value of up to 65 per cent. Getting planning permission for land is also extremely speculative and you should never invest with big ideas about

Land price increases from 2003 to 2006

Land prices in England and Wales		Land prices in Scotland
Price index from 2003 to 2006		
Farmland	47% increase	47% increase
Mixed	53% increase	54% increase
Hill	53% increase	30% increase
Dairy	50% increase	52% increase
Arable	42% increase	41% increase
Year-on-year price index 2006		
Farmland*	20% increase	8% increase
Mixed	22% increase	12% increase
Hill	11% increase	5% increase
Dairy	22% increase	7% increase
Arable	18% increase	8% increase

* Farmland prices increased in England and Wales from £3,121 per acre in 2005 to £4,602 per acre in 2006 and in Scotland from £2,538 per acre in 2005 to £2,737 per acre in 2006.

Information supplied courtesy of Bank of Scotland Agricultural Land Price Index; see www.hbosplc.com for updates

The pros and cons of investing in land

Pros	Cons
• Can be a very tax efficient benefit. Investing in farmland can be free of some income tax and capital gains tax (CGT) and either 50 per cent or 100 per cent of inheritance tax, depending on certain rules and regulations.	• If you buy land (as opposed to investing via a fund), it will need costly and regular maintenance.
• If you do gain any additional planning, returns can be 200 per cent or more.	• Adding value by gaining planning permission takes a long time and is very difficult to get.
	• Large areas of land can be high maintenance and involve a lot of conforming to regulations.

what you will do when the planning permission is granted and a fortune comes your way. Remember that this is unlikely to happen in the short term unless already applied for by the current vendor, in which case it will be priced accordingly. Only invest your cash in land if you won't miss the money at any stage.

Jargon buster

Capital gains tax (CGT) Tax on profit from selling certain assets, not including your main place of residence

Inheritance tax Tax possibly due on some gifts you make in your lifetime and on your estate when you die

TYPES OF LAND INVESTMENT

Within the planning system, land is defined as retail, commercial or residential, but that is for building on, as discussed in the previous chapter. Instead, this chapter concentrates on investing in open space land, of which there are also three types: farmland (or agricultural land), woodland and greenbelt.

Farmland

There are several categories of farmland, including pasture (for grazing), arable (for growing crops), hill (moorland) and mixed (for grazing and crops). The farmhouse, the farmyard and any agricultural buildings are normally considered to be agricultural land as well. Income can be generated from farmland by renting the property

 The Bank of Scotland land price index is at www.hbosplc.com (search the 'press articles' section). Other farmland surveys can be found at www.rics.org (environmental and land section) and www.savills.co.uk/rural/ (news and research).

and/or the land to another farmer or farmers and eventually may, of course, be sold on if the price increases, allowing you to make a return from your investment. This may be to a neighbouring farmer or a new tenant. You can also attempt to get planning permission to develop some of the land and/or farm buildings, but unless the property already comes with permission, this is not something you should count on in your plans, nor do on your own. Not only is there some resistance to developing farmland, but many farmers are already clued into this type of property investment and will already have tried it themselves or will sell at a level that considered this in the price.

Woodland

Woodland is either an area of countryside covered in trees or other woody vegetation such as bushes and shrubs, which can be purchased as an amenity for conservation purposes, or a commercially managed forest, which can generate revenue. The money that you invest is twofold:

- There is one price for the land that you have bought.
- An additional valuation based on the crop that is growing on it and the revenue it can generate.

If you buy commercial woodland, you need a substantial acreage in order to fell and sell enough timber to make it financially viable. There are, however, limits on how many trees you will be allowed to remove each year, and you are not allowed to fell trees without a licence (see box, opposite). There are, however, other ways to make money from woodland, including:

- **Producing and selling charcoal.**
- **Renting out the land** (with permission from the local council) for camping, although this can be restricted.
- **Using the woodland for paintballing,** shooting and other outdoor pursuits.
- **If there is a lake,** you could use it for fishing (subject to conservation restrictions).

All these ideas might require planning permission, which can take time and money and won't necessarily add lots of value to the land.

> **!** Don't buy woodland assuming you will get permission for a change of use - it may not be welcomed or desirable and so you should always have contingency plans.

 For more information on purchasing woodland, go to www.woodlandowner.org.uk, www.forestry.gov.uk (see their booklet 'Felling Trees, Getting Permission') and www.upm-tilhill.com, which also has a Forest Market Report and 'Investing in Woodland' booklet.

Woodland as an investment

If you are considering buying woodland as an investment, it is more likely to be a 'lifestyle' investment with some tax advantages, rather than a major money spinner, although timber prices are starting to rise, so it is possible to make money. However, there are some issues it is important that you are aware of if you decide to become a woodland owner:

- You need to obtain a licence from your local Forestry Commission if you wish to fell any trees or you could be fined £2,500 or more.
- You are likely to need the help of a 'woodland consultant' to help you understand the required maintenance and issues. Visit www.woodlandconsulting.co.uk and ask your regional Forestry Commission.
- You need to manage your woodland, which can cost a great deal every year. If left to manage itself, it will go into decline and not regenerate.
- Timber can take forty years to reach economic maturity so you need to be aware that investing in woodland is a particularly long-term undertaking in comparison to other forms of property investment.
- Watch out for large commercial forests that are being sold in lots. These can be problematic if there are too many owners and not enough overall management. Beware, too, woodland that is being sold by unscrupulous owners who fail to declare that they have been served a notice to replace felled trees. Use an experienced legal representative who knows how to check for these legal obligation, which would become your responsibility upon purchase.

Bear in mind, however, that the income you earn may not be annual, as trees and other woodland income generating products normally take a lot longer than a year to grow. As a result, the money comes in 'cycles' such as five, ten or even twenty years.

Greenbelt

The Campaign to Protect Rural England (CPRE) (www.cpre.org.uk) defines greenbelt land as that which has been specifically designated for long-term protection from development. There are continual stories in the media of greenbelt land being under threat or granted use for residential development due to the pressure to build as many houses as possible. Government targets for housing over the next few years have brought this issue in to the spotlight again, but it should be remembered that there are only 14 areas of the UK designated as greenbelt, which cover just 35 per cent of the land. This means that there is 65 per cent of non-greenbelt land with further potential.

Land banking investments

Many companies buy huge plots of land at agricultural prices and then do nothing with it to raise the land's value, just sell the plots at a profit with the idea that some time in the future planning permission for property will be given (note that these are not plots on which you can self build).

This may seem like a particularly attractive opportunity, not least because the sums involved are relatively small, usually between £10,000 and £20,000. In addition, you may well be offered a 'discount for buying on the day', which can be as much as 20 per cent. The companies selling on plots of land will frequently also have professionally produced marketing packs with an attractive artist's impression of what the plot will look like once planning permission is granted, but beware of such seductive advertising.

What you should consider is that if this is such a fantastic business opportunity, what are they doing offering you this chance? Why are they not keeping it for themselves? They very rarely tell you the answer – unless it's in the small print! If you do decide to think about investing in this way, then you need to adhere to some essential dos and don'ts.

Do:

- Request a survey on the land to find out its true current value.
- Speak to the local planning officer and take onboard his/her views.
- Talk to the highways agency about the feasibility of getting vehicle access to the land.
- Get a copy of the Land Registry title deed of the plot you will be buying and use an independent solicitor to act on your behalf.
- Make sure you can sell the plot back to the company (if, say, you need the money for an emergency or are tired of waiting for the investment to pay off), or onto to another seller and understand the process and costs involved of doing it.
- Request a copy of the company's financial position.

Don't:

- Buy on the day you are offered the investment.
- Buy without visiting the plot of land that is being offered.
- Rely on the information given to you by the company selling the plot, or their associates.
- Buy unless you are sure you will never need the money in the future.

So buying on a greenbelt site, assuming that planning permission will be granted, is not something to be done without considering all the facts.

If you buy land that is currently designated as greenbelt – which includes national and local nature reserves, sites of special scientific interest, national parks, areas of outstanding natural beauty, special areas of conservation and heritage coastland – you stand to make a return in excess of 200 per cent of the money originally invested if you can gain planning permission to build and sell on or build yourself (see page 115). However, it is a very risky strategy and should only be considered if you are willing to wait for many years (which could be ten, twenty or even more), and are also prepared to accept that if you sell early you won't sell it on at the same price, or that you might have to sell it on for much less, or worst, won't get a buyer at all.

CRITICAL SUCCESS FACTORS

Unlike other forms of property investment, there are likely to be strict rules as to what you are legally allowed to do with the land once you have bought it. Financing it has equally strict rules and there are also tax implications. Therefore, this form of investment requires specialised knowledge, so get yourself some independent, professional help.

Will you get a return?

Look at all the available ways to make an income from your land, including renting land and property to a farmer, particularly those with land neighbouring yours.

There are other possibilities, too, depending on the type of land and situation, for commercial as well as residential use – discuss any ideas with a rural land agent.

Do you have your advisers in place?

In addition to taking specialist financial and legal advice (see pages 141–2), choose an experienced land agent before you make your purchase. This is preferable to an organisation that just sells plots of land.

Tax is a key benefit when investing in land. It can be one of the most tax-efficient property investments that you can make, but in order to take advantage of these benefits you need to seek a specialist expert adviser who understands the issues surrounding inheritance tax (IHT) and capital gains tax (CGT) (see pages 202–3).

The main gain for taxation purposes is that it is possible for land to be passed on to your heirs entirely free of inheritance tax, thanks to agricultural property relief. The relief that can be gained varies from 50 to 100 per cent, but to get the full relief, the farm needs to be:

- Owned and farmed for two years by the individual applying for relief, OR
- Owned for seven years by the person applying for the relief who has let it to a tenant for farming.

Don't cut corners – you will kick yourself if you are later presented with a large bill for tax that was avoidable.

Have you had a survey done?

Ideally have a survey done before you make an offer. A land survey is much more complicated and in-depth than for a residential property. The surveyor goes into great detail about the quality of the land, its designated uses and the entitlements and support payments that are available to you as landowner.

One element that is particularly important to check is the boundaries. Depending on the type of land, where it is and what it is used for, you may not be able to see anything that defines its borders. There may not be any fencing around all or part of the land and the boundary may be a forest, a road or a hedge. Your surveyor will provide drawings and measurements to indicate precisely where the boundaries are. Ideally, make sure that you attend the survey so you know exactly what you are buying.

Walk the boundaries – or find another means of transport, depending on how large an area it covers and what type of land it is. Walking the boundaries helps you to get a good idea of the area that your land covers. It also enables you to see exactly what it is next to and alerts you to any ongoing maintenance costs.

Who might you sell the land on to?

Investing in land is such a specialist area that it does not attract the interest of large numbers of people, which may seem good news when you are buying, but is not so great when you come to sell. It is therefore important to identify (before you buy) the sort of person you might eventually sell to and make a profit from. If you think that it might be to another investor rather than a buyer with a real need for the land, then this is an extremely risky strategy as there may be nobody willing or interested in investing when you decide to move on.

To be assured of a return, identify an existing market, such as a demand in the area for farmland. If you cannot identify a future need, you risk never being able to sell and therefore never making money on your investment.

Land investments with farm property can be turned into income by renting to farming tenants, but they aren't very easy to find as they are often tied into an existing agreement. However, investing in farming land with property would normally be less hassle than an ordinary buy to let as the farming tenant is likely to be much more independent than an ordinary one.

For more information about buying land in England and Wales, go to www.uklanddirectory.org.uk and www.defra.gov.uk. For land in Scotland, go to www.Scotland.gov.uk and for land in Northern Ireland, go to www.ruralni.gov.uk.

Finance and insurance

It is unlikely that you will be able to borrow money for buying land alone (including woodland and greenbelt). If you are planning on developing it, you could obtain a loan to cover the costs. However, you won't be able to draw down any of the money until you have received planning permission.

COMMERCIAL LOANS

Buying farmland with buildings is a different matter. The type of loan you can take out is similar to a commercial loan and the main criteria are:

- **The offer** will be a maximum of 65 per cent loan to value.
- **Salaried earnings** not associated with the farm are taken into consideration.
- **The term** can be anything from five to forty years.
- It is subject to a minimum borrowing of £30,000.
- You need to produce a budget and cash flow if it's a fully working farm.
- Loans can be taken out on a repayment or interest-only basis.
- A choice of fixed or variable rate, which is up to 2 per cent more than the base rate.

- A full survey is undertaken on the property, as much to protect you as to protect the money that is being lent by the loan company.

Due to the family nature of farming, loans can be passed to other family members. Because the loans are usually fairly high – hundreds of thousands to

Jargon buster

Interest-only loan A loan where you only pay the interest on the amount borrowed over the term of the loan

Repayment loan A loan where you pay off the interest and the sum borrowed at the same time for an agreed period

For more information on specialist finance for farmland-related purchases, go to the finance company AMC (www.amconline.co.uk), or chartered surveyors Humberts (www.humberts.co.uk), Knight Frank (www.knightfrank.com) and www.farmandcountryfinance.com.

millions of pounds – there are few charges associated with the finance that you would normally get with taking out a residential mortgage.

When considering whether you are eligible for a mortgage, the company will be looking at your application in far more detail than for a residential property. The lender will take into consideration the home, any outbuildings, and the different types of land, as well as any additional rights that may add value, such as shooting or fishing. The company will also assess the profitability of the farming business, any rents from tenanted cottages and any farm subsidies that could be applied for.

INSURING YOUR LAND

Land insurance is more complex than that for residential premises as you are insuring for a business. Employ an expert to advise you, but here's an outline of the different types you should be looking at:

- **Public liability insurance.** This is essential if you have land with public rights of way and buyers or commercial vehicles that are visiting the property.
- **Farm buildings and equipment.** This is used to cover the outbuildings and any expensive equipment required to look after the land.
- **Employer's liability insurance.** Essential if you intend to employ people to work on the land/property.
- **Livestock and crop insurance.** Also essential if you are planning to run the farm.
- **Residential buildings and contents insurance.** Just as important as for any residential ownership.

Additional insurance that you may require is landlord insurance (see page 95) should you be planning to rent any of the land/buildings.

❝In addition to residential insurance, you may have to consider cover such as public liability, farm buildings, livestock and crops. ❞

For more information on insurance for farmland and other types of land, go to the National Farmers Union website at www.nfumutual.co.uk, and also visit www.amconline.co.uk and www.farmandcountryfinance.com/.

Finding and selling land

There are many companies and websites offering plots of land for what appears to be a bargain price. They seem to offer a great return but if they look too good to be true, they probably are.

FINDING YOUR FIELD

The best and safest place to look for land is either to approach an estate agent who specialises in agricultural property and land or go to a specialist website (see below). Alternatively, make contact with local farmers to see whether a deal may be done, or look in a farming publication such as *Farmers Weekly*.

There are specialist companies that have experienced specialists who work in the agricultural and land markets. Normally when you buy a residential property through an agent, they are working purely on the part of the seller. However, there are not lots of farmland opportunities available. In fact, currently demand is higher than the number of properties and land available, particularly for small farm holdings. As a result, the rural specialist agents will also act on your behalf, for a cost of 0.5–1 per cent of the final price of the property.

If all this sounds a bit too much like hard work, then you can consider buying into a specific land fund (see pages 36–9). As commercial funds performance fell back towards the end of 2007, some investment companies started to sell land funds. For more information about land funds, visit an IFA.

LEGAL CHECKS

The process of buying land for investment is similar to purchasing residential property, but it involves a lot more paperwork. In addition to the usual checks, you should ask your legal team to look at the following.

The Land Registry

Unfortunately, not all farmland is officially registered with the Land Registry. This means that extra time may be required to get the land registered before you can go ahead with the purchase and become the legal owner – and this can add weeks or even months to the process. Once you have discovered the exact boundaries, make sure you register

 To get further help finding a field visit www.ruralscene.co.uk (sells smallholdings and equestrian properties) and www.fwi.co.uk (Farmers Weekly Interactive).

Land doesn't come cheap

The seller's perspective is usually that the value of land and property will increase in the future; but as a buyer, the view is often held that others will sell at less than it's worth – particularly farmland. The farmer has 200 acres, so surely he'll sell an acre or two at a small cost? What's it to him/her? This couldn't be further from the truth:

- Most farmland that comes up for sale are large farms. Smallholdings with around 10-15 acres of land are few and far between.
- Many farmers that sell (approximately 65 per cent, according to Humberts) are retiring so they want to maximise their sale price, not take a cheap or 'quick' offer.
- If you border onto farmland and want to buy land off the farmer, don't expect to pay agricultural prices. The farmer – and their agent – knows what value it will add to your property and are likely to want four times the agricultural value or more, to recoup the cost of the 'hassle' of selling off part of the farm, the costs they will incur, the amount of paperwork it will generate, tax implications and, of course, they want to profit from it too!
- The land you buy has to be managed – and this costs! Farmland is a 'living thing'; there are animals and plants/trees that die and you need to get rid of them so they don't cause any damage.

these precisely with the Land Registry so that when you come to sell, the process is easier.

Chancel repairs

Ask your legal team to check if there is any requirement to pay chancel repairs, which means that you legally might have to invest in the upkeep of the local church. This could be from a few hundred pounds to a whole lot more, depending on its condition.

“ Having to pay chancel repairs could result in a very large bill. ”

Check your boundaries

As well as making sure, with your surveyor, where your boundaries are, it is important to realise that those boundaries will require some upkeep, for example cutting hedges and mending fences. Taking a look at the boundaries, and their condition, before you buy the land is a good move. If you discover you are responsible for the fence on the left, it is not like replacing the fence in your garden – with several acres this could cost a great deal of money. Make sure you ask for maintenance cost information.

Land contamination

Contamination of land is also something that you should be aware of, particularly if you are looking to buy land for development, in which case you should have soil surveys done. The types of contamination that can occur are from flooding, climate change, chemical spillage (such as diesel), or livestock buried on the farm. Once the land is yours you may be liable for any damage that may occur or to cover costs of safely restoring it.

Grants

Find out about any grants that may be available. Indeed, some farmers rely on grants to make any profit at all from their land. For example, the farming industry currently receives help with their business via the European Union with single farm payments. This is a subsidy that is available for those that run farms that produce crops and food. It can be around £80 an acre and depends on the level of investment that is made to ensure the farm is maintained in a sustainable way. It is paid for agricultural activity and output, so it is not available for other forms of farming, such as 'equestrian'.

SELLING YOUR LAND

There are many options available when it comes to selling land. Some methods are free while others will incur similar costs to selling residential properties –

❝ Be prepared for a wait as selling land can take a very long time; it can even take years. ❞

a commission of 1–2 per cent of the value. The best route depends on the type of development that you are planning to sell. However, be prepared for the major difference between selling land and selling residential property, which is that you may have a long wait. It could take months or even years to find a buyer, especially if the type of land you are offering is not currently in high demand or if it is being purchased for tax purposes rather than to be used.

The first port of call is likely to be the specialist rural agents (see below), who will charge up to 2 per cent commission on the sale price, but they do offer an comprehensive service compared to residential agents, including:

- **Helping to collate the extensive amount of information** you will require to sell the property.
- **Advising on the different ways** of maximising your sale price, such as building commercial buildings, applying for planning to add value, switching certain fields to different uses and going for more EU subsidies.

 For more information on legalties and buying land, go to Net Lawman (www.netlawman.co.uk). For further information about selling land at auction go to www.eigroup.co.uk.

"Get an independent survey done to be clear on just how much the land is worth. "

- Introducing you to the essential buyers, all of who are likely to have been much more carefully screened than they would be for residential.

As well as advertising on specialist websites and in magazines (see above), you can also put up a board on the land, but make sure it is within the planning guidelines. Alternatively, take the more

usual route of selling via specialist estate agents, especially if they already are part of an auction website.

Finally, if you have obtained planning permission to build more than a single property on your land, it may well be worth approaching land buyers directly. Look to see who is building locally and visit the sites of those who are in competition with each other as this may help you to get the best possible price. However, make sure you are clear on how much the land is worth by gaining an independent survey from a Royal Institution of Chartered Surveyors (RICS) qualified surveyor.

Case Study | John and Kay

As a lover of horses, and having just retired, John and Kay decided to invest some of John's pension payout in buying equestrian land for two horses to share with their children and grandchildren. After five years, the work became too much and the grandchildren lost interest in the horses, so John and Kay decided to sell the land and with buying/selling fees coming to £2,370 and an initial investment of £15,000 and sale price of

£25,000, the annualised percentage gain was 8.78 per cent return, on top of the enjoyment of being able to utilise the land effectively free-of-charge during the period they owned it.

Different types of land incur different tax, so it may have been even better to consider renting the land or to gift/leave it to their family. It is essential to check first with a professional adviser what is the best route to take.

Commercial investments

Commercial investments can be a great way to secure long-term income. They are potentially a great deal less problematic than, for example, residential buy to let, and over the last years commercial properties have also made superb capital gains.

Investment choices

According to Clerical Medical's AssetWatch survey, 'Over the past ten years, commercial property has seen the strongest performance with annual returns of 13.6 per cent per annum, or 258 per cent in total. Commercial property has outperformed residential property every year from 2004 to 2006.'

The outlook in 2008 is not as bright as it has been. One of the big differences between the commercial and residential markets is that the commercial market tends to reflect the economic outlook. In 2007, the economy was affected by problems in the US **sub-prime mortgage** market and, added to that, were the severe financial difficulties of the Northern Rock bank collapse in the UK. With a general downturn in the financial markets, too, commercial investments were much less of a certainty from late 2007.

> **❝ The current outlook is not as bright as it was, as commercial markets reflect economic issues and performance. ❞**

Jargon buster

Sub-prime mortgage Loans on a property made to those with a bad credit history

TYPES OF COMMERCIAL INVESTMENT

There are many different commercial investments, so growth returns are very varied. Ways to invest include:

- **Property syndicates and funds** (see pages 42–4).
- **Property companies.**
- **As a buy-to-let landlord,** either for large corporate tenants, such as Boots, or to small/medium-sized entrepreneurs, such as a hairdresser or clothes shop.
- **Buying commercial property for development** through change of use, for example, adding flats above shops or increasing the returns by dividing premises into more units.
- **Putting your ISA investments into commercial property.** Funds are

The pros and cons of investing in commercial property

Pros	Cons
• Returns vary with the level of risk taken, prime property can be relatively low risk, secondary/tertiary can be high risk.	• Tend to require a long-term investment of ten years plus.
• The rent can be assured for 5-30 years, so no six-month maximum tenancy agreements as with buy to let.	• Investigating a commercial opportunity takes a lot of time and skill, unless you join a commercial fund or syndicate.
• Downturns in the market can be ridden more easily than in residential as an office space can be adjusted for one company with 200 staff, to ten companies with twenty staff. Or a retail use property, with permission, can become an office property.	• The investment upfront in considering or comparing commercial property can cost thousands of pounds and take many months.
• Share some or all of the refurbishment costs of building with the tenant if in their interest (subject to planning/building regulations).	• Help can be hard to source. Most commercial agents are used to clients spending millions, so at less than £1 million you are likely to have to pay for their services and then are unlikely to be a key priority.
	• Commercial property is subject to economic downturns, which can lead to long voids.

invested directly or indirectly. Direct investment means that the fund buys the property, such as an office block. Indirect investments are when funds are used to buy shares of companies that invest in property.

- Investing in commercial premises for your own business, especially as part of a self-invested pension plan (SIPP) (see overleaf).

- Investing in real estate investment trusts (REITs), which were set up to be more tax efficient than other funds. Profits are given directly to investors, but the downside is that costs are higher and opportunities are limited (see page 38).

❝Commercial rents can be assured for years.❞

 If you are considering investment in funds or syndicates, seek advice from an experienced IFA as there are times when commercial investment, just like the residential property market, is not the best thing to do. For example, at the end of 2007, some fund managers ignored commercial funds and reinvested money into other investments as reports suggested that commercial returns had hit their peak for the near future.

Self-invested personal pension (SIPP)

With a SIPP you are able to decide which assets to invest in whereas if you have a traditional personal pension, the pension provider chooses the investments for you. Although SIPP investments are limited to certain assets designated by Her Majesty's Revenue & Customs (HMRC), they appeal to experienced investors who want a direct influence on the performance of their assets.

SIPPs cost anything from 2 to 5 per cent a year to run, compared to, for example, a stakeholder pension, for which the charges would be capped at 1 per cent per annum.

You also need to have a reasonable pension pot to make them work, starting at £50,000.

The risks and returns of commercial property vary with the type of investment (see also the chart, opposite):

- **Prime commercial property** is a low-risk investment involving a high input of capital, usually by large institutions, such as insurance companies. The property is in a top spot on the high street in major towns and tenanted by a leading company on a long lease with virtually guaranteed returns.
- **Secondary properties** are small to medium-sized (£0.5 million–£1.5 million) retail, office, industrial or leisure spaces in 'off prime' spots with a good quality tenant, but are easy to dispose of in an average market.
- **The tertiary and small secondary market** is for the private investor in smaller businesses in less important locations. It involves lower capital investment but potentially higher returns and there is potential for added value through refurbishment.

BE AWARE OF THE END USER

Remember that your contacts will be making business-based decisions, not the emotive choices that normally prevail when buying residential property. So bear in mind what types of businesses the property would be suitable for and who is most likely to occupy it. Even more importantly, think how flexible the space is. Would it have a variety of uses?

They may be large enough to attract a successful tenant who will stay for a long time (and may be particularly attractive in this instance if they are flexible enough to be extended) or have the potential to be broken up in to

---

For more information, go to www.aref.org.uk/home.html, www.landlordzone.co.uk and www.trustnet.com. In addition, www.ipf.org.uk/?page_id=115 is a good analysis of the commercial market from an investment perspective.

Commercial property: risk and return

These figures are a guideline to the returns you may be able to gain from investing in different types of commercial property. However, every investment is unique, so always check this information and use these as a guideline of what should be achievable. Each percentage includes rental income and capital growth returns.

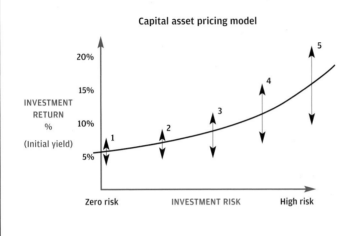

Capital asset pricing model

1 Risk-free investment, such as in a building society

2 Prime property

3 Secondary property

4 Tertiary and small secondary market

5 Property development

Information supplied courtesy of www.LandlordZONE.co.uk

Tertiary and secondary property returns

Adding value, splitting buildings and development	8-20+%
Secondary property: smaller shops and offices in side streets, suburbs, etc.	7-15%
Prime property: large high street shops and offices	4-6%

From 1 April 2008, there is no relief from business rates for empty properties. If a property is unoccupied, you could be stung with a large monthly bill on top of any other loan and insurance payments you need to make. Make sure you're not caught out!

beaten track' or even down a side street just a few feet from the main shopping centre, it is likely to be more difficult to let and consequently worth less from a capital and income perspective. Ideally, look for areas that don't just rely on the general economy of the area to survive – for example, cities such as York have a 'heritage trail' and are therefore attractive not just to local shoppers but to tourists too.

smaller units to suit the needs of a number of small businesses. In this instance, several tenants will maximise the income potential and minimise the risk of having a property left empty.

CRITICAL SUCCESS FACTORS

As with any property investment, buying in the right location is essential and this is particularly significant in the world of commercial property, especially retail which is very much dependent on passing trade. Shops – except where they have a particular niche market and people will seek them out – will not be successful unless they have many prospective customers walking past on a daily basis. If a retail unit is 'off the

Get to know the local economy

If you are looking at investing in industrial or office-related commercial buildings, get to know the local economy. Find out what type of companies and institutions are already there – such as telecoms, manufacturing and science parks – which could be looking to expand and what type of property will be in demand both now and in the future.

Take care not to invest in areas where just one or two industries dominate the market. For example, in Newbury a few years ago Vodafone decided to pull out of all its offices in the centre of town in favour of a brand new facility to the north of the town. As a result, there was a glut of offices on the market at the same time – good news if you were looking for a bargain, but bad news for anyone trying to sell or rent out their properties at that time.

Flexible spaces

Flexibility will always be an important factor in the commercial property market. If in times of economic

❝ For a successful commercial investment get to know the local economy and be creative with your use of space. ❞

uncertainty (and reduced spending) you can change premises from retail to offices or alter one unit into two or three, the probability of maintaining an income from your investment will be much increased. Better still, if it is a shop, for example, it is occasionally possible for the tenants to bear some of the change costs – something that is highly unlikely to happen with residential property!

Be aware of market changes

If you are looking to gain money from investing in new areas, you will need to consider the following factors:

- **Designated government growth zones,** such as Ashford, Peterborough/ Cambridge, Milton Keynes and South Midlands, and parts of London.
- **Population growth,** a key requirement for any return on investment.
- **Changes to the infrastructure,** for example, the relatively new M6 toll road has generated new opportunities in commercial premises near major new junctions.
- **Growth, in particular commercial sectors** or as a result of corporate relocations, for example, government offices such as the Patent Office moving to Newport or the BBC moving offices to Manchester.
- **Impact of tourism on the area,** whether it's growing or in decline.

If you keep a close eye on the businesses you have invested in you

> **!** If you invest in an up-and-coming area, there is a great deal that can go wrong and, crucially, expected earnings may not be in line with predictions in the information from the developer. Consider the fortunes of areas such as Cardiff, which has been successfully regenerated, versus Hull, which is struggling to fill new developments.

can often head off possible problems. For example, the pub industry has changed from solely drinking establishments to places to eat. As a result, some pubs that haven't changed their offering accordingly have gone bust, while others that can't support this service have been sold off by pub chains. If you are looking to invest in this type of business, look at how it can be diversified in order to maximise the investment at best and, at the very least, prevent it from going out of business. Maybe it needs a quick refurbishment and selling or renting to

❝ You should also be aware of changes in population and know that infrastructure affects markets. ❞

a new landlord, or (in advance of purchase) applying for planning permission for change of use to offices or retail units.

The tenancy agreement

If you are buying an already-rented property, ensure the tenancy agreement meets all your criteria and involves nothing untoward. The legal situation with commercial investments is complex and it is imperative that you understand your legal obligations and responsibilities. Although rules and regulations can be made in a landlord's favour, this depends on negotiation with the tenant and they may be effective for 5, 10, 15 or even 30 years – a long time to be locked in to an agreement if you don't like the terms.

The key legislation to keep an eye on is the Landlord and Tenant Act 1954 and you should keep up with any changes that may affect you.

Your advisers

As with all investments, make sure that you have a great team of advisers on hand, including surveyors and financial and legal consultants (see pages 27–32). You should also have specialist advisers if you make your investments in certain industries, such as pubs and restaurants. In these industries there is a history of

people being sold apparently highly profitable businesses only for them to discover, all too late, that the figures on which they had based their purchases were artificially inflated and their investment was worth nothing like they expected. An expert will pick up any figures that appear too good to be true and prevent you making a costly mistake.

> **!** Some industries and services are more profitable than others. New businesses are highly vulnerable, so are more likely to go bust and cost you rental income and more charges in getting a new tenant. Small traders also work on tighter margins and so are less likely to be able to survive a downturn than larger, more established, businesses.

❝ Regulations may be effective for thirty years – a long time to be locked into an agreement if you don't like the terms. ❞

> Publications such as *Estates Gazette* (see www.egi.co.uk) and commercial sections in your local newspaper will help you keep up to date with legislation.

Finance and insurance

There are many ways of investing in commercial property and probably just as many ways of financing those investments. Here, we look at your options and then move onto the all-important subject of insurance.

If you invest money in syndicates and funds, it is likely you will put in a lump sum, which will be from £20,000 to over £100,000. Some of these funds and syndicates will borrow against the money that you have put in, while others will use the money to gear the investment and borrow more money to invest in bigger projects.

FINANCIAL OPTIONS

If you are buying a commercial property for residential development, the financing will be similar to that on pages 117–20. There are two other forms of financing for commercial premises:

- Finance to buy commercial premises for your own business (known as owner occupier).
- Finance to buy commercial property to rent or sell on to others (known as investment).

Finance for investing in commercial premises has some similarities to residential, but the underwriting process is very different in that every deal is considered on an individual basis according to the circumstances of the borrower, what the building is to be used for and whether the borrower/occupier already has a background in that particular industry.

Talk to an experienced commercial finance broker who can approach a broad range of financial institutions to try to get you the best deal once he or she has established your exact requirements. Ideally, look for brokers that offer more specialised and detailed advice on the actual property itself. This may even include negotiating the purchase price on your behalf with the commercial agent.

Finding a broker

Ideally, a broker should belong to the National Association of Commercial Finance Brokers (NACFB) as finance for commercial properties is not regulated by the FSA. The NACFB is a trade organisation that has a third-party complaints procedure. Its website is www.nacfb.org. See also the following commercial property websites: www.commercialplus.co.uk, www.cpfconsultancy.co.uk, www.landlordmoney.co.uk and www.mortgagesforbusiness.co.uk.

The type of information a lender or broker will be looking for includes:

- **Full customer profile** and background of all the borrowers including details of any personal accounts and personal borrowings, such as mortgages and loans. This would mean all directors where a limited company is involved and any and all partners.
- **Financial and payment records of any tenants** and full details of the current legal agreement, including covenants. This is particularly important as the likelihood is that you will purchase an already tenanted property and any lender will be more interested in a tenant's ability to pay, payment record and any risks involved rather than your earnings.
- **An independent market value of the property** by a commercial surveyor, which will include the condition of the property and details of the lease terms.
- **Some evidence of a successful track record in property investment.** A first-time investor will find it more difficult to raise finance at more competitive rates and may need to include other forms of security such

as his or her house or a buy-to-let property. Loan-to-value levels may be restricted to below 70 per cent and rates may be as high as 2.5–3 per cent over bank base rate.

- **Actual and potential rentals,** either from current tenants or recommended by the surveyor, or both.

Lending criteria differ from property to property depending on the project, but the following terms are likely:

- Loan of up to 75 per cent of the property's value.
- Rate of 1–3.5 per cent above base rate.
- A mortgage term between 10 and 25 years.
- Money lent varies between £25,000 and £15 million, or more.
- Loans are normally based on variable rates although some fixed rates are available for smaller loans (for example, between £250,000 and £1 million).
- Loan payments can be repayment, interest-only, or a mixture.
- More favourable terms are available for longer and better tenancy agreements as well as for more established blue chip clients.

Covenants and commercial legal agreements

Covenants for commercial properties are restrictions on a building's use, or they set out defined boundaries for the tenants of commercial premises. As a landlord, you may need to include a covenant in your legal agreement, but as a tenant you need to ensure that there is not a covenant in place within the lease because this may restrict your plans for the property.

The cost of obtaining a loan

Costs for all commercial loans are more expensive than residential. Legal fees are around three times higher than if only bricks and mortar is being purchased. Valuation fees are also approximately twice those of a residential deal. The lender may also charge an arrangement/broker fee of between 1 and 2 per cent, depending on how much is being borrowed but this is generally negotiable. However, there are some changes in the market place and hence the fees are becoming more competitive. If the lender/broker do charge, make sure that the service you receive makes the extra cost worth it.

Arranging a commercial mortgage

Investing in a commercial property for your own business is very similar, but the main difference is that you will be the tenant. The lender will consequently concentrate on your company's accounts and give preferential rates to companies that have three or more years of robust accounts, a trading history, a good level of profitability and other assets, as this will help to ensure that you can continue to pay the lender in bad times as well as good.

Commercial lending criteria tend to be more favourable for owner-occupiers than investors:

- Lending up to 85 per cent of the property's value, although this depends upon individual circumstances and if there are any other assets the loan can be secured against (for example, your own home).
- Rates of between 1 and 2.75 per cent above bank base rate.
- Borrowing a minimum of £25,000.

- Loans are typically based on a term between 10 and 25 years.
- Fixed and variable rates are available as are interest-only periods.

COMMERCIAL PROPERTY INSURANCE

Insuring a commercial property is similar to insuring a residential leasehold property. You have the choice of insuring the building and its contents. But if you are only a landlord and not in occupation, you would only need to insure your buildings and can recover the cost from your tenants.

Unlike residential, however, you are unlikely to be able to obtain a quick 'online' calculation, as much will depend on the commercial activities being undertaken in the building. For example, restaurants and fast food outlets are high risk due to the possibility of fire. A factory handling and processing flammable materials and chemical products would also attract a much higher insurance premium than an ordinary office.

157

To apply for an insurance quote to cover the building alone you will need to have the following information to hand:

- **How much it will cost to rebuild the property.** This information will be supplied by a specialist building/ structural engineer (who has professional indemnity insurance should any errors occur), your surveyor or the commercial agent involved in the sale. You will find this figure in the valuation report.
- **Type of commercial activities** that will be undertaken and detail of any potential hazards such as fire and chemicals.
- **How many people will be working in the building** and whether they are there for 24 hours a day or just during normal working hours.
- **What the building is made of** (for example, brick, concrete) especially walls, floors and the roof.
- **Whether there has been any flooding or subsidence** – and if you want this type of insurance.

- **What security measures protect the premises,** such as 24-hour personal security, type of alarm system and safety features, such as sprinkler system, locks on windows/doors.

The insurance will include a three years' 'loss of rent' feature, and this covers you should there be a physical problem with the property and your tenants have to move out. This should not be confused with losing rent through non-payment by a tenant. You will need to consider additional insurance if you want to protect the property from terrorism.

In addition, if you are planning to do any development work on the building, you may well need separate cover in case of related accidents.

Make sure that any changes to the property are passed by the planning and building regulations office. Keep all issued certificates as you will need to produce them both for insurance purposes and when you come to sell the property.

Cover your liabilities in one quote

If you are buying the building and running your business from the premises, it is worth getting a quote for all of your business needs, including public liability insurance, at the same time. Insuring the liabilities separately may well cost more than insuring the whole business with a single policy.

 For more information about commercial insurance, visit www.assetsure.com, http://business.hiscox.co.uk, www.landlordmoney.co.uk and www.mortgagesforbusiness.co.uk.

Identifying good investments

Finding a commercial property to invest in is not an easy task. It's not like walking into a residential estate agency and getting a list of properties then working out on your own whether your choice is going to be a good investment or not.

FACTORS TO CONSIDER

As many commercial investments will require a higher cash input than residential it is really important to discover whether there is an established demand for tenants. Unlike residential buy to let, it's much more usual to purchase a commercial building with tenants than without as the longer the tenancy and more established the tenant, the easier it is to get finance. This is particularly true when it involves a large national or multinational company such as Halfords or Boots, for example.

What are local purchase prices like?

To find out what the market is like, use comparables and get help from a commercial surveyor or a smaller commercial agent. Auctions are good places to look for properties to buy (see pages 67–9), but you will still need help before making an offer – and it's especially important that you don't go over any offer recommendations as the capital growth of commercial property often takes longer to materialise than with residential property.

Make independent checks

If you see a property that looks like a bargain, be cautious. Check whether there is a problem with the tenants or if the legal agreement is an issue. It might be that there is something happening, such as a new development, that will negatively affect the price. Some more unscrupulous people have taken on commercial properties – such as a pub – put in a tenant and then artificially created 'high yields' that makes the property look more attractive than it is in reality. Inexperienced investors have bought the property in good faith and then lost a large part of their investment value because they failed to make such checks.

SURVEYING A COMMERCIAL PROPERTY

In the commercial property arena many commercial agents are also surveyors, and this qualifies them not just to find you property but sometimes to give accurate valuations on property. The work they undertake – and which you pay for – is much more than a residential surveyor would do and as a result the valuation fee is much higher too.

A commercial surveyor's role

A surveyor checks many things, including:

- Putting a value on both the property's sale price and estimating rent.
- Reviewing the lease agreement.
- Preparing a Schedule of Condition, which records the condition of the property prior to occupation.
- Carrying out rent reviews and lease renewals.
- Preparing a Schedule of Dilapidations, which records the condition at or near the end of occupation and is used to enforce repair and maintenance obligations on the tenant.
- Negotiating between landlord and tenant where any dispute arises. In this situation it is common for both parties to engage their own surveyor.

Landlords of commercial properties should use the Full Reaping and Insuring (FRI) leasing agreement and it is an essential part of a surveyor's role to check that your lease has the necessary FRI clauses. With this type of agreement,

Buying commercial property for your business

If you are buying property for your own business to work from, it is worth checking out all the costs that would be involved when running the property to ensure you look at it from a business perspective. These will include:

One-off costs

- Stamp duty land tax

Purchase price	Rate
£0–£150,000	0%
£150,001–£250,000	1%
£250,001–£500,000	3%
£500,001 and over	4%

- List of repairs and alterations that are required.

Ongoing costs

- Business rates (check what would be applicable via the Government's website: www.voa.gov.uk).
- Running costs (commercial costs of heating and lighting are much higher than for residential).
- Annual service charge if you share facilities such as parking and/or roads with other companies.
- Loan finance and mortgage costs.

Assessing commercial property investment

✓ Tenant demand: make sure it's there; do some market research.

✓ Buying with existing tenants: ensure due diligence undertaken of both individuals and company and have the leasing agreement checked by a solicitor or surveyor.

✓ Location: preferably in a good trading location and improving area with good transport links, and, if possible, with something extra about the area to sustain business – tourism, for example.

✓ Realistic rental income and rental growth predictions: get good rent comparables.

✓ Realistic property value estimates.

✓ Building integrity: get the building checked structurally.

✓ Realistic financial calculations with a built-in margin of safety: do a cash-flow forecast.

✓ Calculate what the investment is worth to you and don't pay much more, especially when bidding at auction.

✓ Get the financing in place.

✓ Don't overstretch yourself financially: start off small and build up gradually.

✓ Do some pre-tax planning: think about the long-term tax implications of your investment – get professional advice before you invest.

✓ Flexibility of use: think about alternative and potential uses, possible planning approvals and what would happen if you lost a tenant?

✓ Understand the legal aspects (Landlord and Tenant Act 1954) and get a good solicitor with appropriate property experience.

✓ Don't skimp on leasing costs: a good lease will cost £500–£1,000 but will make sure you are protected as a landlord for almost any eventuality. You should be able to get the tenant to share the cost 50/50.

✓ Know your responsibilities as a landlord and learn how to manage tenants competently.

Checklist supplied courtesy of www.LandlordZONE.co.uk

If you are a tenant of a commercial property, with full reaping and insuring (FRI) clauses, make sure you have a building survey done first to ensure you aren't liable to put major building defects right, even though they were there before you!

bankers and/or any other participating funding parties.
- Checking the commercial property lease.
- Possibly renegotiating with the current tenants to reflect your wishes rather than simply continuing the agreement that the tenant had with a previous landlord.
- Handling the financial side of the business, including organising deposits and the drawing down of commercial funds from your lender.

the tenant rather than the landlord is responsible for all internal and external repairs to the property while the landlord's main responsibility is only to insure the buildings. Even then, the insurance costs can be passed on to the tenant, making any initial outlay minimal.

LEGAL CHECKS

The process of buying and selling commercial property is, in essence, very similar to buying a residential flat as it may involve buying the freehold and checking leases and tenancy agreements. However, it is essential to use a solicitor experienced with commercial property. The legal side includes:

- Checking the title of the property.
- Carrying out searches.
- Answering any questions raised by

If you are buying property to develop, your legal adviser will also help with advice on planning issues, gaining planning consent, creating clauses in an agreement, such as taking an option on land/premises subject to planning, and also creating agreements required in respect of joint venture agreements with a third-party funder.

Organise time with your adviser to go through all the legal documents. Take a list of any questions you may have with you and what you want to do with the property from an investment perspective. It is also essential that you understand what can go wrong and what to do if tenants don't pay so that you know how much money you should keep aside to cover any void or default payment periods.

For further information on the legal side of making a commercial investment, go to www.commercialplus.co.uk or telephone Easier Commercial at 0845 4600 800.

Selling your investment

There are two main ways of selling a commercial investment that you have rented out to tenants: via an agent and via an auction room. Ideally you sell the property when rent and the property's value is at its highest, so yields are good.

You can also approach organisations such as the East Midlands Development Agency, which often have departments to help and encourage companies to move to an area, including sourcing suitable premises, and may have someone interested in your property.

There is little compromise available to the would-be purchaser/investor of commercial property – it's either exactly what they want or it doesn't suit them at all – so it may take some time to sell unless you are very lucky and can sell to an existing tenant, for example. However, unlike in the residential market, properties are usually sold already let, so you don't have the complication of getting tenants out in conjunction with managing the completion.

CHOOSING AN AGENT

There are different types of commercial agent. As with residential, they range from the large corporate company that has offices all over the country to smaller businesses that focus on your local area.

Work with a commercial agent who is used to selling the type of property that you have. It is no good giving an office building to an industrial specialist, or indeed a £150,000 property to a company that is selling sites and complexes worth millions of pounds. Instead, go to commercial agents and discuss similar properties that they have sold in the last six months. Ask the following questions:

- Did the properties sell for the asking price or less?
- If less, by what percentage?
- How did they get buyers?
- What business networks do the agents have?
- Is there anyone on their mailing list who would be interested?
- Do they have investors who might be interest in buying into a new, exciting opportunity?

The cost of selling

The cost of selling via an agent or auction room will vary – and will be negotiable. Commission will be slightly higher than the residential market at around 2.5 per cent of the premise's sale value.

163

BE PREPARED

In view of the time it can take to sell commercial property, ensure your legal and surveying contacts have prepared all the paperwork for sale and then the property can be advertised through an appropriate commercial agent or through the auction process.

❝Check your legal and surveying contacts have got all the paperwork ready so the property can be marketed efficiently.❞

Case Study Gerald and Christine

Having looked at the various options in investing in property, Gerald and Christine had researched the local market and taken their time to look at which type of investment would give them the best return. They noticed there was a mix of residential and commercial properties being sold, which meant they could let the commercial property to cover the cost of renovating the residential units. These often just needed a small refurbishment to add value before being let.

The income from the commercial investment was £350 per month and after a gap of three months to refurbish the flats, the two flats let at £500 and £550 per month, giving a total income of £1,400. Over five years, the total income received was £80,850, with mortgage and other ongoing payments adding up to £72,000. This gave a gross income of £8,850 over the period. More importantly, though, they sold the two flats and the shop for a total of £315,000.

This gave a return before tax of £315,000 sale proceeds minus:

> £220,000 purchase price
> £10,000 renovation costs
> £13,305 purchase/sale fees

The total is £71,695 plus £8,850 income = £80,545. So the gain from an initial investment of £45,305 (includes £22,000, which is 10 per cent deposit on the purchase price of £220,000) is 35.5 per cent per annum.

Tax implications on commercial and mixed-use properties are complex and beyond the remit of this book. Always seek specialist advice.

If you have bought into a commercial property syndicate or fund, see pages 42-4 to see how you can sell them.

Investing overseas

With increased globalisation, each of the ways that you can invest in the UK is also possible somewhere overseas. However, buying and selling abroad is an extremely tricky way of investing in property. Many companies give the impression that 'it's easy money', and for them it might be. For you, the reality of getting it right is very different.

10

Opportunities abroad

Many people abroad joke that there are three prices for a property: the price for locals (the lowest), that for property investors abroad, and then the price at which they sell property to people from the UK (the highest).

Part of the reason for this is that apart from capital cities, the price of property overseas seems to represent a great bargain in comparison to the UK. Companies selling investments abroad (many ex-timeshare salespeople) are also used to taking money from the British, who are often seen as gullible. Sadly, many fail to check properly what is being bought and don't use independent advisers to check that their purchase is the right one for them.

There is a mountain of information about 'investing abroad', unfortunately much misleading, and little in the way of accurate information to enable investors to compare deals, particularly between different countries. Much of the information is not independent, coming from the salespeople themselves, many

 It is imperative, as with all investments, to seek out experienced and independent advisers to enable you to check that any information you are given is accurate, and that there is a market to sell on to in the future.

Sources for assessing overseas investment

www.doingbusiness.org: a website from the World Bank that includes forecasts of countries' economic and population growth and the demand and supply of property.

www.globalpropertyguide.com/: an independent site giving a country an 'investment rating' and information on such things as costs, tax, legals and financing.

http://investors.assetz.co.uk/property-investment-tracker.htm: gives a tracker chart that includes the costs of buying/selling property and typical yields. Also forecasts what will happen to property prices and estimates returns.

www.ipd.com: information on the Global Property Index.

www.knightfrank.com: in 'research reports' read the latest 'Global House Price Report' and 'Global Real Estate Markets'.

Property price and rental returns around the world

These are examples of top performing areas around the world to give you an idea of different returns available when compared to the UK. They are based on a square metre and yield basis for buy to let and on a potential capital return on properties bought and sold. The returns are affected by many things, mostly supply and demand together with other factors described in this chapter. For more information on prices and rental yields visit www.globalpropertyguide.com.

Potential buy-to-let income returns for 2007

Tahiti	15%
Egypt (Cairo)	11%
Slovakia (Bratislavia)	10%
Argentina (Buenos Aires)	8%
Germany (Berlin)	5.4%
UK	5.4%

House price growth (adjusted for inflation) for 2007

Singapore	24%
Estonia	15%
Norway	12%
Australia	8.6%
Sweden	8%
UK	7.5%

of who are not regulated in the way that a UK company might be. So, if investing abroad is something that appeals to you and you can afford the time and upfront investment, go in with your eyes wide open. Check and double-check your facts, if you have any doubts, check again – and never let your heart rule your head!

INVESTING ABROAD VERSUS IN THE UK

One of the main reasons why investors are starting to look abroad is that it is harder to find opportunities in the UK that 'stack up' financially. Buy to let is more difficult to gain a return on, unless you can buy below market value. Finding a renovation project is like looking for a needle in a haystack.

However, in some areas abroad it is possible to gain better yields and achieve capital gains last seen in the UK around 2000. However, you must still allow for the vagaries of a market that depend on a property's uniqueness in terms of location and condition. Average

167

The pros and cons of investing overseas

Pros	Cons
• Big gains available if you are willing to take a risk in emerging markets, however, this comes with a high risk.	• Higher investment cost upfront, such as flights.
• Investing at a lower level than in the UK while still gaining good returns.	• Can be high risk in areas where property law is not well established.
• Can enjoy property for holidays or later in life.	• Restrictions on mortgage lending and taking money out of the country.
• Opportunity to spread risk across several countries' economies.	• Often more costly to buy/sell abroad than in the UK.
	• More complicated as rules can be changed overnight, and there is a different language and culture.
	• Property is more likely to suffer from natural disasters than in the UK, which can ruin your investment.

prices are a useful guide when comparing investments but not a good indication of the return, which you might get from an individual purchase or investment deal.

TYPES OF OVERSEAS INVESTMENTS

There are so many ways of investing overseas that it is impossible to cover all the possibilities here. So identify a country or specific investment, for example, renovating in France, then seek specific shows, magazines and internet sites (see page 213) to find out as much as possible about the different options that are available. We can, however, explain the work needed for each type of investment, irrespective of which country you buy in. The critical success factors described on

pages 170–5 are similar wherever you buy. But the rules, regulations, timings and returns are likely to be very different and these are what you need to identify.

Property funds

If you haven't got the time or expertise and don't want to spend months pouring over economic data and flying around the world to check out how good an opportunity is, look at property funds. These are a possible way of diversifying your portfolio if you have other property investments – see pages 36–9 for more details on choosing a property fund.

Buying off-plan

In some countries it is possible to flip properties by buying off-plan (see page 46) and then selling them on. However, this can be hazardous. In a major area for development, other new properties may become available and be more aggressively marketed than yours, taking away demand from your investment. The slowdown in the UK property market has also caused some people who have bought off-plan abroad to lose their deposits or take out expensive bridging loans (see page 94) as they have been unable to sell in time.

Worse still, people who haven't investigated developers carefully enough have found that their property has either not been built or that the building work is not to an acceptable standard. Being able to get your money back in this type of situation is something you may take for granted in the UK, but in a foreign country you may have little or no recourse. Before you pay out any money, check that the builder is insured so that if they do go bust you have a way to recoup your hard-earned savings. It is also essential to make sure that the builder has the correct certificates to build on the land, that the land and your ownership are correctly registered and that the property has received the building regulation sign-off.

Renovation and new build

As already established, these are not easy tasks at the best of times and in a foreign country you are at the mercy of their planning laws and building regulations, which may or may not be well documented. Some rules can be purely local and it may be down to the Mayor to officiate. It is imperative, therefore, that you get the correct

information and permissions for everything, including any changes you wish to make. Don't rely on your builder as you are the one to suffer if you don't do it right.

Make sure all permissions are in writing, but remember that documents are unlikely to be in English, so employ an English-speaking but local, independent legal adviser to make sure

❝Some rules can be purely local and it may be down to the Mayor to officiate.❞

Dealing with builders abroad

This can be something of a lottery. They may be fantastic – better and cheaper than in the UK – or they may end up taking your money and not doing the job. Not all countries have strict building regulations and tradespeople do not necessarily have to have qualifications, but check first.

- Follow the advice on pages 75-7 in line with the country's contract terms.
- Be aware how long everything may take. For example, it may take months or even years to obtain a building approval certificate just to get started and getting utilities connected could take a year or more.
- For any repairs carried out, particularly major renovations, pay someone to track, report and manage progress, or make sure you are there daily.

all your documentation is in order. This applies before and during the buying process until the project is completed.

Buy to let

With buy to let it is important to carry out the due diligence set out on page 161, but there are many other considerations when buying abroad. These include:

- Who will pay for repairs?
- What currency will the rent be paid in?
- What are the legal options if you have a problem tenant or letting agent?
- When you are not there, how will you know when the property is being let? An unscrupulous agent may take rent and tell you the property is empty.
- How do you pay the bills?
- What is the situation regarding tax?

- Who will look after the property if you are ill?
- Is there anyone reliable to do any maintenance?

Many questions, all of which need answers before you go ahead! It will certainly give you peace of mind if you have someone on the site who you can trust and have known for a while or who has a legal responsibility to you (see below for finding an agent).

CRITICAL SUCCESS FACTORS

Although yields and returns may look very seductive, as does the idea of making money from letting and selling a holiday home in the future, even before you visit a country, you need to be aware of the following factors.

Timescales

Buying and selling a property in the UK takes on average around five months. However, abroad it ranges from weeks to years. Depending on local demand and laws, it may be much more difficult to buy and sell than in the UK.

Costs

Although house owners in the UK frequently complain about the cost of moving, there may be a nasty shock in store when you go abroad. Some

---

Pay a visit

Visiting the countries and the developments that you are interested in is essential as you can get to know the locals as well as the area.

- Visit several sites and check on information in person that you have previously gained second-hand.
- Check whether quoted prices are inflated 'international' prices rather than local ones.
- See what businesses are in the area, whether they need property (and what type) for their staff.

 Look for agents who belong to organisations such as the Association of International Property Professionals at www.aipp.org.uk.

countries make a charge similar to VAT when purchasing a property and some agents charge over 10 per cent to sell your property. Additional costs can turn a bargain into an expensive mistake. So plan an accurate budget that takes into account all those hidden charges, plus ongoing costs.

Overseas tax systems

We all have some understanding of the UK tax system. Our main residence is free of any capital gains, but a second property would attract capital gains tax (CGT) when we sell. However, taxes abroad are completely different, even by region. This is further complicated by the fact that some countries have tax agreements with the UK, so make sure you seek independent advice and fully understand your tax liability of buying, selling and any annual tax you may need to pay as a property owner.

Professional experts

As well as using a local legal professional, employ one or two international lawyers who are independent of the country that you are investing in. Ask the same questions of each lawyer so that between them you should get the correct information. For example, when establishing who owns the property, one lawyer may come back with one name while another may find

out that it is actually owned by a whole family. Some experienced investors and investor clubs work on this basis to avoid legal difficulties later down the line.

Foreign currency exchange

It is incredibly important to understand and sort out exchange rates and charges before you look to invest overseas. Your holiday money may be your only previous experience, which at the most, might be a thousand pounds. However, when buying abroad, the cost of converting your sterling to purchase a property and then converting it back again after sale could lose you a large part of your profit.

Working with a specialist foreign currency provider can make an enormous difference to the money you pay out – and what is finally returned to you. Their expertise is to plan to have the right amount of foreign money when you need it – and at the best price. Always compare what your bank may be offering to what you can get from a currency specialist.

Be aware, too, that there are rules on how much money you can take out of a country to the UK. Not all countries allow you to take your money out and/or may limit what you can take out annually.

There are two ways in which you can purchase your foreign currency – a spot contract and a forward contract (see over).

For more information on how to buy your currency and currency rates, go to www.currenciesdirect.com, www.moneycorp.com and www.travelex.co.uk.

- **A spot contract,** which is when you purchase currency now for immediate use. This process normally takes around five working days.
- **A forward contract,** which takes more planning. This is where you can arrange to buy the currency at the current rate for delivery up to two years ahead of time (especially useful when buying off-plan). You will need to pay a 10 per cent deposit upfront and the remaining balance will then be due when you need to send the currency overseas.

> **❝ The political and economic climate of the country where you are buying may not be stable. ❞**

A specialist currency company can also save you a fortune in bank charges when you purchase the property and if you continue to own the property.

The changes in a country's economy

When buying abroad, don't forget that you have little control over the future of that country. In the UK, at least there is an opportunity to vote and the political and economic climate is stable. So always be aware of potential problems that can occur abroad, which will affect your investment. You will have heard horror stories, such as people who bought in Spain and then had to pay a developer for the privilege of taking part of their garden to build a road! There are many other issues that can affect your property

---

Finding a foreign currency provider

- Look for companies that are happy to break down the one-off and ongoing costs of money transfers.
- Ask what charges will be made when you buy and while you own the property.
- Ask if they will guarantee that there will be no bank charges when you transfer monies into an overseas account.

Typical charges made by currency specialists are a one-off transfer fee, which could be as little as £15, and if you need money to be transferred on a regular basis this can cost as little as £4 per transaction. Compare these to any charges your own bank may make, which are likely to be significantly more.

 For more information about the rules, regulations and risks associated with property ownership, see the *Which? Essential Guide* to *Buying Property Abroad*.

investment. For example, in Thailand, the Government decreed that overseas ownership of property was dependent on the developer having a Thai resident partner owning the majority of the company. In some countries one person may sell you their land and if the legal work isn't done properly, a few months after you've completed you could find out that the property is owned by ten other family members – and they want it back!

To prevent falling into similar traps when investing abroad, do your research, get independent advice and hire specialist international property lawyers to act on your behalf.

Keeping up to date

You can keep up to date with overseas investments via internet sites and magazines (see below), and also through the property press, such as *The Sunday Times* property section, *The Daily* and *Sunday Telegraph* and *The Express* as well as shows such as the Property Investor Show (www.propertyinvestor. co.uk). Other helpful programmes are *Selling Property Abroad*, and if you have cable TV or internet access, you can watch property programmes all day from www.realestatetv.tv/site/home/.

Established versus emerging markets

An established market is one that was started or set up long enough ago (this could be anything between two and twenty years) and sufficiently successful to suggest likely continuation or permanence as well as having established property prices and rentals that you can compare. Examples of established markets would be countries such as France, the UK, Canada and Italy – basically countries where the political and economic climate is relatively stable. The benefits of an established market are:

- Price information is more consistent, making it easier to work out the potential return from an investment.
- There is an established system of legal ownership and registry of properties and land, including planning and building regulations.
- You are likely to be able to gear your investment via an international mortgage.
- There are established agreements in place with regard to the movement of money in and out of the UK.
- There are established tax treaty agreements.

❝Hire specialist international property lawyers to avoid traps.❞

For magazine websites, go to www.homesoverseas.co.uk, www.brooklandsgroup.com and www.property-investor-news.com. Other useful websites are www.aipp.org.uk, www.assetz.co.uk, www.channel4.com, www.globalpropertyguide.com, www.lawoverseas.com, www.propertyfrontiers.com and www.propertysecrets.net.

- **Supply and demand for property,** for example, is there enough people to rent your holiday let, or tenants to rent all year round, or someone to sell it to when you want to cash in your investment?

The downside of investing in an established market can be that, depending on the type of investment you find, property price growth and yield is typically lower than riskier markets.

An emerging market is a country in the early stages of economic development and is expected to grow rapidly. Examples of emerging markets would be Turkey, Brazil and Vietnam. These countries are starting to grow and gain some level of political and economic stability.

> **!** An emerging market can experience not just economic and political setbacks, but also natural disasters that would not happen in the UK. Imagine, for example, a war breaking out in your chosen country or an earthquake or flood. You could end up losing your property altogether, or tourism could be affected so much that, without rental income, you couldn't continue to fund your investment.

Emerging markets have the benefit of a major influx of international funds. International businesses move in to take advantage of economic growth in the country, bringing money with them. As a result, local people get richer, so they spend more money and, in turn, boost the economy.

There are some great opportunities to make money from property in emerging markets, But, as with any high investment returns, there are typically high risks associated with this strategy and you have to be prepared to put in an enormous amount of leg work – including travelling to the country, visiting different areas and spending a good week or two either investigating individual property investments or checking out opportunities that companies are trying to sell you.

As with areas of regeneration in the UK, sometimes the expected demand just isn't there. Prices are set early with off-plan deals, some costing only a relatively small amount, but two years later when you are committed to buy there may be nobody to rent or sell to.

This has happened in some areas of Bulgaria where properties just don't have the demand that was originally forecast. In some countries, such as Dubai, most of the immediate money has probably been made, and the questions for future returns are: what happens when the building stops? Will the expected influx of investment continue? If it does, will values then hold, increase or decrease due to over supply?

Spotting an emerging market

Spotting emerging markets is a job for economists and property experts and your task is to discover who you think does this well and then take their lead – easier said than done, of course! However, most experts agree that the following indicate emerging market opportunities:

- A legal change that allows overseas ownership/investment. For example, formal land registration of all properties/land; agreement for overseas mortgage funding.
- Changes to communication routes. For example, the growth in low-cost airlines in and around Europe; joining two countries by a bridge or tunnel.

- Better facilities, such as a consistent supply of essential utilities: electricity, water and gas.
- International investment, such as multinationals moving in.
- Joining an international or regional community, such as the EU.
- Growth in demand for the country's resources, for example, the growth in Aberdeen when oil was found.

Understand potential future demand

Whichever market you decide to invest in, it is essential to understand the current and future demand for property within that market. For example, take the island of St Lucia in the Caribbean and compare this to Cape Verde, which is being tipped as the 'next Caribbean'.
If you wanted to buy in St Lucia, you would go to the local estate agents to view property. They would then take you to land or property that would only be sold to foreigners due to the price it could attract – the kind of prices that many of the locals are unlikely to be able to afford.

The way the locals buy and sell property is through their own network. Properties for locals (which, of course,

may not be on the more expensive beach fronts) would cost from as little as £60,000 for a two- or three-bedroomed property.

If you look at Cape Verde, prices of property being sold to international investors are not that different to those that a local would pay for property in St Lucia. However, there are no established resale or rental markets in Cape Verde, so you've no real idea of a potential investment return.

A long-term, more sure-fire investment abroad (not just a holiday investment) is likely to be one that is bought at 'local' rather than 'international' prices and where there is a ready made (or likely to emerge) resale market to purchasers from the local community as well as from abroad.

175

Finance and insurance

When organising finance overseas, you can invest money from your home or other properties that you own. Alternatively, you can borrow against properties purchased abroad, although the latter option is not possible in every country.

IMPORTANT DETAILS

Before moving onto the details of raising finance, there are some important matters you need to be aware of:

- Discuss your personal and financial circumstances with an IFA or an experienced mortgage expert in overseas finance.
- Establish how long it takes to obtain a mortgage abroad. In the UK, it can be done in up to six weeks, but in other countries it may be three months or more. This is important to be aware of if you have to complete quickly.
- Decide if it would be beneficial to get a 'loan agreed in principle, subject to valuation' from a foreign bank, which is much like a 'mortgage agreement in principle' in the UK. It might speed up matters once you find the property you would like to invest in.
- If you have or are planning to have children, it is important to understand the inheritance laws in the country in question. In some European countries the laws state that your property will be disposed of in accordance with their regulations if you die during ownership, unless you have/can make separate

legal provision. For example, in France, 50 per cent of your property has to be left to your children or their children. Whereas in Portugal, inheritance tax has been abolished.
- In certain countries, such as the Czech Republic, you may have to set up a company to own a property, or invest with a local citizen.

❝ Consider factors such as how long it takes to get a mortgage abroad, the type of finance available, plus laws on inheritance and property ownership. ❞

MORTGAGE CRITERIA

It is important to be clear about the criteria for lending in different countries as it will affect your ability to gear your investment and therefore may mean the difference between investing in one or several properties.

Minimum deposits

In the main, just as with a buy-to-let deal, most countries require between a 10 and 20 per cent deposit. These include countries such as France, Spain, Canada and South Africa. However, there are some countries that require more, for example, Bulgaria, Turkey and Germany need approximately 25 per cent, and in Cyprus it can be as high as 40 per cent.

Minimum loan amount

Most mortgage lenders and brokers have a minimum amount that you can borrow, usually from around £20,000 to £50,000 and may be as high as £125,000. This may not seem to be a problem compared to buying in the UK, but in some countries this would represent serious finance for quite a large and/or expensive property and there may be no demand from the local community to buy it, so your market will be limited to international buyers only.

Mortgage term

In the UK, it is normal to take out a 25-year mortgage but other countries vary considerably on what is allowed. In Israel, the usual term is from 3 to 15 years and in Greece, it is up to 25 years. Others may extend the borrowing to last for as long as 40 years.

Some mortgage lenders/countries will give you more favourable terms if you borrow in their currency as opposed to Sterling, Euros or US Dollars and will vary the term depending on whether you take out a repayment mortgage or an interest-only mortgage.

Repayment and interest only

Lenders may offer interest-only or repayment options or a mixture of the two. One area that is different abroad is that in some countries, particularly in Europe, lenders fix the interest rate for the full term of the mortgage. As a result, you know exactly what you will pay every month while you own the property, which is excellent for budgeting. However, as in the UK, be aware of any early redemption penalties, which could eat into your profits if you pay earlier than the lifetime of the mortgage.

Special requirements

Some lenders can access specialist mortgages for land or buy to let, while others won't allow you to borrow for renovation work or other individual requirements, or will charge you a higher interest rate and/or arrangement fee if they do.

Mortgage interest rates

These can vary dramatically and move up and down within a matter of months or a year. In general, interest rates in Europe, outside the UK, are around 5–6 per cent. Places such as Cape Verde are around 7.5 per cent and South Africa is as high as 11–12 per cent.

Currency

Lenders abroad may put restrictions on which currency you can borrow in and this is likely to be Euros or US Dollars. Others will allow you to specify the currency you want for your mortgage.

UK mortgage versus an overseas mortgage

This table describes the pros and cons for remortgaging a UK property to buy another abroad versus taking out a separate mortgage to buy overseas.

Remortgaging a UK property		Separate mortgage on overseas property	
Pros	**Cons**	**Pros**	**Cons**
• May be cheaper if you stay with existing lender. • May negotiate cheaper lending for existing loan. • No currency risk.	• Puts your main home at risk. • Costs: valuation of UK property, legal fees. • May be more expensive than a foreign loan.	• Less risk to main home. • Potentially lower interest rates. • Keeps administration of overseas property separate.	• Ongoing currency risk. • Administrative complications of transferring money. • Can be difficult to find a lender.

Age limits

Bear in mind that all lenders in all countries give some restrictions on the age that you can borrow up to. For example, in Malta you cannot borrow over the age of 65 years. The standard age limit is 70 but in some countries it is possible to extend that to 80 years.

> **" Most UK international banks, IFAs and some specialist companies offer mortgages overseas, so you can and should compare deals. "**

SOURCES OF FINANCE

There are many sources of finance for overseas property investment (see box, opposite), but whichever you choose, it is important to get independent advice before proceeding. A developer may offer to give you an introduction to a mortgage company and to legal advice to enable you to buy off-plan from them. However, such arrangements should be independently checked as the advice and assistance may not be in your interest and the third party they introduce you to may even take commission (without telling you) from the developer.

Most UK international banks, IFAs and some specialist companies now offer mortgages overseas so you can and should compare deals. With the right loan-to-value ratios and the best interest rates, you can maximise your profits and potentially buy more than one property.

Sources of overseas finance

UK banks

Not all UK banks provide loans for overseas finance. Here is a list of those that do:

Barclays: www.barclays.co.uk/buyingabroad/
HSBC: www.hsbc.co.uk/1/2/personal/travel-international/buying-property-overseas
Abbey National, international division: www.abbeyinternational.com/

These companies typically only invest in certain countries, such as France, Spain or Malta, and may have expensive currency charges, so check any deals offered with specialist overseas mortgage lenders and currency exchange companies.

Specialist mortgage brokers

Some companies deal solely in organising mortgages for people who want to buy abroad, and ideally you should look for a finance company that has at least ten years experience in that country. This gives the company an opportunity to have built good relations with lenders and understand what can be done and use trusted partners.

These include companies such as Conti Financial Services Limited (www.mortgageoveseas.com). Other companies that specialise in overseas mortgages include www.assetz.co.uk and Savills Private Finance (www.spf.co.uk/). Also ask your IFA for advice. To find a specialist, go to www.unbiased.co.uk.

The costs of financing a mortgage abroad are not that different to those of a UK mortgage:

- An arrangement fee, which can be as high as £500 or 1 per cent of the loan value.
- A broker's fee, which is usually up to 1 per cent or more of the value of the mortgage.

Shop around and compare costs of different lenders as you may well be able to pay much lower charges that will boost your potential profit.

Dotting the 'i's

- As you are buying property for investment purposes, establish whether you can remortgage the property when it increases in value, and how much this will cost you.
- You also need to ensure that the lender is aware this is an investment and that you may require the monies to make the property habitable, rent it out and/or extend. If they don't know this, they may not offer, or they may charge a higher percentage.
- Check for any redemption penalties you may incur if you want to sell your property before the end of the mortgage term.

INSURING YOUR PROPERTY ABROAD

Insuring property abroad is very similar to insuring property in the UK, although terms and rates can be very different and more costly. In addition, there may be exceptions that may not apply at home.

Your mortgage lender will almost certainly offer you a quote for your building and contents insurance, but this may not be the best policy, or the best value. One major issue, particularly with holiday lets, is that the property may be empty for periods of time and as this can negate a policy claim in some circumstances so you must make sure you are covered. In some countries you may be expected to install high levels of security or get better insurance cover if the property isn't in a gated development.

If you are planning to rent out the property, the types of insurance you might need are:

- Public liability.
- Employer's liability if you have, say, a housekeeper and pool attendant. This might also be necessary to cover tradespeople.
- Accidental damage cover.
- Insurance to cover lost rental income, for example, as a result of a cancelled holiday booking.

Obtain a policy that is written in English and any exclusions should be clearly listed. The excesses that apply are an important consideration as there may be more claims than normal if you have tenants and you should also find out the excesses in the event of natural disasters such as earthquakes. According to HiFX (an independent currency exchange broker), storm damage and burst pipes rank as the more frequent claims.

If you are taking out a mortgage, life assurance will be required – and you may be compelled to take the chosen lender's in-house scheme. As usual, ask for quotes from different companies to get the best cover available at the best price. In some cases, a lender's insurance for property can be 45 per cent more expensive than buying it independently, so if a lender does tie you in to other products, make sure these don't make the total deal uncompetitive. Visit your IFA and get quotes from your mortgage lender as well as specialist insurance companies (see below).

❝A major issue can be if the property is empty for periods of time, which can negate a claim. ❞

 For more information on these insurances, see page 120. The websites for specialist insurance companies for overseas properties include www.hifxinsure.com and www.schofields.ltd.uk.

Finding an overseas property

Unless you have a good idea of where you want to invest, it's a tricky task to search the world for the top property investment! This is made harder because what and where you want to buy may not be the best idea from an investment return perspective.

WHERE AND WHY TO INVEST?

You may want to buy a property that you can also use as a holiday home but the best returns may come from a commercial property in an inner-city area. Your heart may say, 'Renovate a property in France' while your head knows that a house or flat in Poland would bring much greater rewards.

Different property investments therefore require looking at different locations and they need to meet different criteria. For example, a holiday home is likely to be somewhere rural or by the sea, with a pool and a terrace. Even with the help of an agent, holiday lets can be hard work due to tenant turnover and if you have invested in an 'up-and-coming' area, by the time you want to sell and reap your rewards, there may be a glut of newly developed properties on the market – making yours look five years out of date.

So, be very clear about your objectives: is the property merely a money-making venture or do you want to incorporate some of your own needs and compromise on the potential returns? Whatever your decision, don't narrow your choice to one area and a few properties. Check out different countries and look at similar investments in each one to work out what gives the best overall return. To narrow your investment choices, consider:

- **Where in the world is forecast to give the best returns?** Use investment trackers, comparison websites and forecasting reports (see pages 167–8).
- **Understand what it is about the country (and an area within that country) that is causing prices to rise** and look at the relationship between capital gains from property and the income returned. Work out whether these changes will have a short- or long-term benefit and narrow down the options to suit your time frame.

❝Don't narrow your choice to one area and a few properties too soon. Keep your options open.❞

- **Look at economic and population reports.** Ideally you want a country that has an increasing population, growing wealth and demand for private renting and ownership, while having a limited amount of space to build more homes.
- **Check the historical and predicted interest rate movement.** Just a few per cent can add hundreds of pounds to your monthly costs and turn a profit into a loss.
- **Look at the currency rates,** most specifically the historical, current and forecasted changes. For example, at the end of 2007 it was a good time to buy in the US while £1 was worth $2. If the dollar were then to improve against the pound, profits would increase on selling the property.

Once you have narrowed down the countries you want to investigate further, you should compare:

- **The ease and cost of access** plus the research costs.
- **Buying and selling costs.**
- **The costs of setting up** and investing through a business rather than as an individual.
- **The finance costs** and gearing potential.
- **The legal ownership of land and property,** how robust it is, whether the country's rules are more biased towards the landlord or the tenant, together with what rules are specific to an overseas owner versus a resident of that country.
- **If a holiday let,** find out how many weeks you are likely to be able to rent out for (consider holiday periods, climate, local customs) and actual values.
- **Ongoing management costs** for buy-to-let properties.
- **Costs, timescales and local rules/regulations** for development and renovation.
- **Taxation** on your income and capital gains, other taxes and inheritance rules.
- **The likely length of time** that you would need to hold the investment to get a return.
- **Possible future changes** that may help to increase the value of your investment, such as better communications (especially flight and port), changes in the law (such as properties becoming mortgageable to locals), or changes in culture (for example, a culture of renting changing to a culture of buying).

Identify what market you are going to be selling to in each country and work out which is likely to be the easiest to exit from.

Useful websites that will help you find property include www.findaproperty.com, www.fisksinternational. co.uk and www.rightmove.co.uk.

HOW TO INVEST?

You have several options for finding the opportunities you are seeking.

Property investment 'finders'

These are people who take a brief from you on your budget, the sort of return you are looking for and where you would like to invest. Some specialise in certain countries or regions and have contacts there who will obtain shortlists of what is available and arrange to show you round. Others produce fully costed 'property offers' that they sell to their network, which you can be a part of. The benefits are their knowledge, the downside is that they can be very expensive.

If you do decide to use property finders/companies make sure they have a good reputation and are members of an organisation such as the Association of Relocation Professionals (ARP) (see below). Some companies are set up by property investors who are already investing in certain areas and earn money from sharing their experience with others.

Property investment clubs

Some property investment clubs (PICs) work extremely well for investors but as they tend to specialise in certain countries or certain types of investment, be aware they are trying to sell you what they

 When viewing a property, it is essential that you take precautions such as letting other people know what you are doing and, if you have any doubts, hire a car and follow the agent to the property.

have rather than all the best deals available globally. Never feel pressurised to buy, especially by deadlines, and always visit the properties/countries before making any decisions. There is more information on PICs on pages 198–201.

International property agents

To find a reputable agent, look at the following organisations:

The Association of International Property Professionals: www.aipp.org.uk
European Confederation of Real Estate Agents: www.webcei.com
World Properties: www.worldproperties.com
The International Real Estate Federation: www.fiabci.com
Team Abroad: www.teamabroad.com

 The website for ARP is www.arp-relocation.com. Other websites for property investment companies are www.county-homesearch.co.uk, www.homesearchcostablanca.com and www.property-venture.com.

Ten common mistakes when investing overseas

You know when you go on holiday and the local dish or drink tastes fantastic, then you bring it home and somehow it just tastes awful? Well sometimes it is exactly the same when buying property overseas.

1 Not considering who the property can be sold to, to make a profit.

2 Believing figures given by the sales team and not independently checking them.

3 Buying a property without visiting the area and the property or land it is to be built on.

4 Choosing services that are provided by the company selling the investment opportunity, such as mortgage and legal advice, and not organising independent expert checks.

5 Not seeking specialist tax advice prior to investing in property.

6 Poor insurance cover in countries where natural disasters can happen, such as earthquakes or floods.

7 Not having an independent survey on the property, most importantly from an expert who speaks English fluently and can also write well in English.

8 Not taking enough time and money to consider all opportunities within a country.

9 Lack of appreciation of the time it takes to get the required permission to buy/renovate/let a property. In many countries you will need an EU card, or an 'alien' licence for overseas property buyers before you can purchase anything.

10 If required to sell a UK property to fund overseas investment, pricing the UK property too high and not selling in time to complete on the purchase.

Estate agents and other 'local' experts

There are good and bad local agents and experts everywhere. An agent will be keen to sell you what they have on their books but may have no contract with the vendor in some countries. They can therefore be reluctant to give you the property details to take away from their office as they are not protected from you doing a private deal with their vendor. As a result, they are likely to want to take you to view the property themselves.

Do it yourself

If you are an experienced investor, this can be a good option, but if you aren't, then take your time and check all the possibilities carefully. Go to a wide range of developers and agents and, if you can, find someone you can befriend, preferably through a recommendation rather than meeting in a bar. However, beware of fraudsters who will be looking to line their own pockets. Always surround yourself with independent experts prior to making an offer and exchanging on your property.

CONSIDERATIONS FOR OVERSEAS PURCHASES

It is important to be aware that in many countries you can't just turn up and buy a property. There are specific rules and regulations that you need to adhere to.

Permits and other requirements/restrictions

Several countries require you to have a permit or licence to be able to buy and/or let property and some even have rules specific to the region. Make sure you are clear on the costs and time involved to get your licence. In St Lucia, for example, an 'alien licence' is required to buy land/property. This can cost around £1,500, take months to secure and requires fingerprints and checks to confirm that you don't have a criminal record. In Brazil, you need to officially register with the Government and have a tax identification number called a 'Cadastro de Pessoa Física'.

Leasebacks

These are schemes that are most popular in France but also available in

66 There are good and bad local estate agents and experts everywhere, so always make checks and go for independent advice. 99

 If you want to terminate your leaseback deal, you have to let the management company know at least six months before the renewal date, or you may find yourself automatically signed up for another nine years.

> **❝ Leaseback deals are increasingly popular, but invest for at least nine years to make it viable. ❞**

countries such as Turkey. You buy the freehold of the property and then lease it back to a management company. They take over the management of the let, doing everything from furnishing it to finding tenants, collecting the rent and paying the income to you, typically on a quarterly basis.

Leasebacks are available via resale, but many are sold from new and benefit from not having to pay the 20 per cent VAT sometimes due on new property. The income is guaranteed, normally between 4 and 6 per cent, and you can spend time in the property without having to worry about maintenance. The downside of the deal is that it should be considered as a long-term investment for a minimum of nine years as you will probably need this long to make the most of capital growth.

A recent change in the law has made leaseback deals even more popular. Previously the VAT discount had to be paid back if you sold before owning the property for 20 years but now as long as you sell to someone who keeps the leaseback option, you don't have to.

However, reservation fees can be high (up to 5 per cent) and while you are only being paid quarterly, the mortgage payments will still be due on a monthly basis. In addition, if in one year a high percentage of owners want to sell their properties or they cease to become leasebacks, the management company may have a clause that says you have to pay a full year's rental income to the leasing company. Also establish what happens if the management company goes bust. It could be the case that someone else takes over and increases the costs.

Holiday bonds

A holiday bond is like a property syndicate, but it can have tens of thousands of owners. It is similar to

 Always get a scheme such as leaseback or a holiday bond checked out by an independent solicitor and never rely on information provided by the people you are buying from, or their associates.

 For more information about leasebacks, see www.assetz.co.uk, www.selectfrenchhomes.com/ and www.propertysecrets.net. For holiday bond information, go to Holiday Property Bond at www.hpb.co.uk.

a normal financial bond except that the investment is purely in property and they are designed for enjoying the benefits of holidays abroad in the company's properties rather than for investment purposes. A one-off fee buys points that entitle you to rent available properties at a cost. In some cases, bonds can be passed on to children when you die.

LEGAL CHECKS

Not many people in the UK market concern themselves with the legal side of purchasing property and tend to leave everything to their solicitor and/or conveyancer. If there are problems, it is usually possible to sort them out without too much difficulty.

However, when buying abroad, you should be a great deal more cautious, especially when there can be questions over the legal ownership of property. You could lose both your property and the money invested and may spend additional cash on court cases that can go on for years, costing a great deal of money. The key services for which you will need to use a legal representative overseas are:

- **Advice** on that country's laws on buying, selling and, if required, renting or developing, together with how long the legal process might take.
- **Advice about grants** available for overseas investors.
- **How land and property ownership works.**
- **Making sure the person selling the property is the sole legal owner.**

‘‘ When buying abroad be especially cautious with regard to the legal aspects of your deal. ’’

- **Checking all contracts and agreements,** from developers if buying off-plan to buying from a local selling his or her home to you.
- **Liaising with the officials in the country.** Some have specific representatives, such as the notary in France, who carry out the official work connected with your purchase.
- **Ensuring that all the necessary legal documents** and certificates required to build or change the property are correct and independently verified.
- **Liaising with the mortgage company** with regard to the monies required and also to advise you on the lender's conditions.
- **Ensuring you can let a property** if you want to and that you have the correct

> **!** You may also need legal services to check contracts and the sale of timeshares, holiday clubs, property bonds and properties being purchased through investment clubs, funds and SIPPs (see page 195).

Where in the world to invest?

It's hard to work out where to invest around the world and everywhere you read about is usually sold as a 'hotspot'. However, as with different types of property investments, there are different countries that will be suitable to help you achieve your investment objectives. Furthermore, different companies are always likely to recommend different areas – as well as some that are the same – depending on their research and expertise.

Here are some different recommendations, in alphabetical order, for forecasted growth in different countries in 2008 and beyond. Make sure that you investigate any country's and individual property's potential investment risks and returns before you invest your money.

Assetz
Brazil
Cape Verde
France: Brittany, Languedoc
North America (USA and Canada)
Turkey: buy to let in Istanbul

Property Frontiers
Argentina: Buenos Aires
Brazil: Natal, Sao Paulo
Canada: Fort McMurray
Slovakia: Kosice
Uruguay: Montevideo, Punta del Este

Global Property Guide
Argentina: Buenos Aires
Bulgaria: Sofia
Columbia
Egypt
Uruguay

Property Secrets
Bulgaria: Sofia, Varna (but not the coastal area)
Czech Republic: Brno, Ostrava, Prague
Poland: Gdansk, Katowice
Romania: Bucharest, Brasov, Cluj
Slovakia: Bratislava, Kosice

For more information about areas to invest abroad, go to www.assetz.co.uk, www.globalpropertyguide.com, www.propertyfrontiers and www.propertysecrets.net.

---

paperwork to do so. Some countries/regions require a licence to let/renovate property.
- **Understanding what happens with regard to your inheritance** and making a will.
- **Setting up a trust or a company** (for example, offshore), if required.

- **Dealing with any disputes** with neighbours, the local authorities or developers selling property.

Legal representatives can also take care of local or national paperwork that you may have to submit on an annual basis.

Selling abroad

One of the key considerations to be aware of is that it can take up to two years to sell, rather than the average three to five months that it takes in the UK. So make sure that you research the selling process of the individual country BEFORE you buy, so you can plan well in advance about cashing in your investment.

MAIN CONSIDERATIONS

The first thing to consider before you put your property up for sale is who is likely to buy it, as this will help you decide who to sell your property through. If, for example, you are planning to sell to someone else in the UK, look for a British agent that deals with selling property abroad. If, however, you are looking to sell your property to someone local, then go to a local agent. Ensure they are members of a professional organisation and check any terms and conditions with an independent, English-speaking solicitor. Follow the same process that you would in the UK (see pages 78–81), but you need to identify the differences specific to the country you have bought in.

- If you want to sell to someone who is likely to be a tourist, look at selling during the tourist season rather than in December when there are less likely to be buyers around.
- Be aware of the cost of selling abroad. Although we think UK agents are expensive, agents abroad can charge a lot more. For example, in the United States you pay 3 per cent commission on the price of the property being sold; in Portugal, agents fees can be 5–10 per cent.
- Get the price of the property right and place it with the right agent. It's no good just putting it on the market for what you want to sell it for, so research the market, as outlined on page 25. Once you have identified who is selling similar types of properties and an idea of the price you may achieve, then it's worth calling in local experts to value the property for you.
- Ensure that you discuss the legal requirements of selling and are aware of the various stages of the selling process. If you are based in the UK, far away from your property, it is essential to know if you need to be present in the country at any stage to fill in and/or sign documents to pass the ownership over to your buyer.
- Put up a 'for sale' sign outside the property so locals and passing tourists can see the property is for sale.

Be sure to list a number to call to book an appointment. Every country, and potentially region, will have their own way of advertising property. They may have property papers or magazines, or advertise in local shops. In Australia they often have an 'open day' for potential buyers organised by an agent, which sometimes includes the incentive of a barbecue! And if you want to sell to the international market, you can even advertise privately in generic overseas magazines that cover many areas, or specific ones that might cover, for example, France or Spain.

- **Consider foreign exchange rates** (see pages 171–2).
- **Be aware of any rules and regulations** relating to taking potentially large sums of money out of the country you are selling in.
- **Understand any tax implications and payments** that you are required to pay, both in the country where you have bought and the UK.

 Try not to let people you don't know into your property or take viewings alone as there is the possibility they may be looking at it to see what you have in the house rather than being a genuine buyer.

** Bear in mind foreign exchange rates, rules and regulations on moving money, and tax implications. **

 For more information about investing overseas, see the *Which? Essential Guide to Buying Property Abroad.*

Property and pensions

Pensions and their performance have been the source of much debate in the media for some years. The previous weakness of the stock market compared to the more buoyant property market has led to around 25 per cent of all adults (according to research by Mintel) investing in the buy-to-let property market as a way to save for the future.

Meeting your pension needs

How much do you need in your pension pot? Is it there already and, if not, can property investment help you achieve it? These are some of the most important decisions any of us are faced with.

Before you decide to invest in property to help fund your lifestyle in retirement, you need to see how much you have in the pension pot already:

- **Check your state pension** (see below). If you retire before 6 April 2010, you can get a full pension forecast from the Pension Service, but for others the full service is not available until Autumn 2008.
- **Talk to your HR department** if you have a company pension, and ask to see the latest estimates of what your pension will be worth. They may put you in touch with the IFA who deals with their investments.
- **Confirm the details of any private pension schemes** that you may have invested in.

Once you have taken these steps you will have a much clearer picture of what your pension pot is likely to be. You then need to work out how much more may be required to fund your retirement. Read Chapter 1 (pages 9–20) to understand what level of risk you are happy with. Do you prefer a high return from a high-risk investment, or a low return from a low-risk investment, or a mixture? Normally the longer you have until retirement, the more feasible it is to take on higher risks, particularly where property is concerned. Whatever you plan, always check with an IFA who specialises in retirement planning (see also the box, Be aware of the risks, opposite).

It is difficult to determine exactly how much you will need in the future, but assuming that you have paid off your mortgage at retirement, think about the following points:

- Do you want to stay in the house that you have now?
- What is the cost of running your home, including utility payments, refurbishment/maintenance and insurance?

It is important to get a pension forecast. To check your state pension, go to www.thepensionservice.gov.uk/atoz/atozdetailed/rpforecast.asp. For more about the Proudential research, go to www.pru.co.uk/content/presscentre/.

- How much do you pay for everyday living, such as food and clothes? Include in your calculations presents, holidays and spending.
- Make allowances for an emergency fund for illness and to pay for help in the house and garden.

According to Prudential, the average cost of living for retired households in the UK will rise to around £33,619 per annum in 2011, and this figure is higher for those over 75 years. That's a lot of money to find each year.

When investing for your retirement, you need to be thinking about two things: the income you need to live on and any lump-sum payments required. With any personal current pension scheme you will be able to draw down monies from the age of 50 (prior to 6 April 2010) or 55 (post 5 April 2010). Normally you can cash in 25 per cent of your pension scheme as a lump sum and draw an income from the remainder for as long as you live. When you die it may be possible for the remaining fund to be used to provide an income for a dependant, such as a surviving spouse, and/or provide a lump sum for a beneficiary, such as children or other family members.

> **" When investing for retirement, you need to think about two things: income and lump-sum payments required. "**

Be aware of the risks

You should be aware that there are risks associated with investing in property for pension purposes. To make sure you have an income or make the capital gains that you need it is important to diversify your investments and not put everything into property. The risks of relying solely on your property investment include the following:

- You can't access your money for many years as you need to invest in property for the long term to get a reasonable return.
- There might be times when you can't rent the property or there are long void periods. Will you still be able to survive financially?
- You might not be able to sell the property in the year you want to retire.
- If you are trying to sell during downturns in the market, there may not be much profit left after tax.
- The properties you have chosen might not grow at the rate you hoped for.
- With regard to any pension, it is wise to use a mixture of different investment routes rather than just rely on one single one, such as one buy-to-let property or trading down from your own home, to fund your retirement needs.

WHY AND HOW TO INVEST

The benefits of investing in property to fund your pension, if you get it right, are substantial:

- **Greater flexibility.** You don't have to wait until you are 50/55 to draw any income/lump sum.
- If you cash in a lump sum, you don't have to invest in an annuity – you can spend or reinvest it as you like.

193

- Easy to pass down to your family/friends via a will.
- Can reduce your family's inheritance tax bill (see page 202).

If you want to gain income in retirement in the future from your property investment, then it's worth considering:

- **Buy to let:** ideally paying off as much of the capital as possible so you pay a low mortgage or none at all and gain more of the income in retirement, or sell to give you a lump sum to reinvest in other income-generating investment vehicles.
- **Build to let:** this gives you rental income on average at a lower cost than if you had bought a property already built.
- **Holiday let:** this can give you some additional income as well as cheaper holidays if it is somewhere that you like to stay.
- **Income generating property funds and syndicates.**

❝ A holiday let can give you some additional income and cheaper holidays, should you want to stay there. ❞

If you are thinking of moving abroad when you retire, it is worth considering buying a property now if you can afford it, know the costs involved and before prices rise. You could rent it out as a long-term let or a holiday let and then move in when you're ready.

Another strategy is to work towards paying off the mortgage on your own home by a certain date to enable you to retire on time, or even early. If you invest in property over a period of ten years or more, for example, and sell at a profit and buy something smaller, you can use this money to help reduce or pay off your mortgage.

TAX BENEFITS

What you don't always get from property (unless you invest wisely and with professional advice), but do get with a pension, are tax benefits. If you are currently a basic-rate tax payer (22 per cent, reducing to 20 per cent from 6 April 2008) and want to invest £100 a month in a pension, you get tax relief, which means that you only have to invest £78 a month (£80 from 5 April 2008) and Her Majesty's Revenue & Customs (HMRC) puts in the rest. If you are a higher-rate tax payer (40 per cent), you still pay £78 and claim the additional tax relief via your tax return.

However, there is now a compromise available to allow you to take advantage of tax benefits and invest in property at the same time, via a self-invested pension plan (SIPP). Although originally intended for all types of property, including residential, changes to the rules mean that SIPPs are currently only used for commercial property investment. Other ways of investing in property are through REITs (see page 38) and/or property trusts.

The self-invested pension plan (SIPP)

With a SIPP you can make your own investment choices (for example, from specific stocks and shares, government bonds and unit and investment trusts) rather than leaving this to a fund manager. This allows you to control your investments, enabling you to buy and sell property, if you desire, within the fund without incurring the same income tax or capital gains that you would normally be liable for outside a SIPP. You can't use this to avoid paying tax on property trading activities. You can either pay to have your pension fund managed or you can manage it yourself, but if you choose to pay, you may incur high charges. Check this before you make a decision.

SIPPs are for experienced investors and those with large pension funds. Although you can borrow against the pension fund, the amounts you can borrow are not that high. You can only usually afford to use a SIPP to invest in property for your retirement if you already have quite a substantial pension pot. For example, if you own a company and have your own commercial premises, you may want to put the property in your SIPP as the rental income and capital growth will then all be tax-free. However, you can only borrow 50 per cent of the property's value through your SIPP, so if

Property held in a SIPP

Below is an example of how you can save tax by investing property in a SIPP as opposed to buying one or two buy-to-let properties to fund your retirement.

Purchase price: £100,000.
Held for ten years and increases in value to, say, £200,000 and then disposed of.

- Capital gains charge in SIPP: £0.
- Capital gain out of SIPP: £18,000 (assuming the CGT allowance has already been used).

The SIPP would have annual charges of approximately £500, so there would be a total cost over the ten-year period of £5,000. Therefore even after deducting the charges of £5,000, the tax saving is still £13,000, if held in the SIPP.

Rent would be paid directly into the SIPP, so there is no income tax and the rent would increase the overall value of the SIPP. If the property was held outside of a SIPP, any rent would be taxable.

The downside of investing in a SIPP is that only 25 per cent of the SIPP's fund value can be taken as cash, whereas the whole of the property sale figure, after CGT could be taken if held outside of a SIPP.

Information supplied by Derek Jordan of the St James's Place Partnership (www.sjp.co.uk)

195

the property is worth £100,000, your pension pot would have to contain a minimum of £50,000 plus associated buying or selling and managing costs before you could 'afford' the property.

If you don't have a enough funds in your pension pot to invest in property via a SIPP in full, it is possible to put part of the investment, such as 25 or 50 per cent of the property in the SIPP while the rest is subject to the normal rates of income or capital gains tax (CGT). Alternatively, you could invest in a fund or in a specialist 'syndicate SIPP', which allows you to invest at a lower level, around £30,000 or more, to buy specific commercial properties as part of a group of individual investors.

❝ SIPPs are for experienced investors and those with large pension funds, but it is possible to put part of the investment into one. ❞

For more information on SIPPs go to www.moneymadeclear.fsa.gov.uk/products/pensions/types/self-invested_personal_pensions.html, www.jameshay.co.uk and www.sjp.co.uk. For a property SIPP calculator go to www.invidion.co.uk/sipp_property_purchase_calculator.php.

Your property portfolio

Passion is key to investing in property, but you also need to build up your portfolio in a hard-headed and sensible way, making sure you consider tax implications.

Building your investment

There are two ways of building your property investment portfolio:
you can either do it yourself, or you can work with specialist property
investment clubs that will bring property investments to you.

There are upsides and downsides of both and you need to work out which is best for you. At the same time, you need to ensure you research the tax implications BEFORE you invest in any property or expand your portfolio being clear about the likely tax implications of the investments you are making.

PROPERTY INVESTMENT CLUBS (PICs)

Property investment clubs (PICs) can seem particularly appealing to the inexperienced investor. They offer a way of gaining knowledge about investing in property while spreading the risks involved. Some offer to 'educate' you at a cost ranging from free to thousands of pounds and others 'discount' properties for purchase.

If you are busy and inexperienced, this kind of service can seem very appealing as the alternative strategy of looking for opportunities yourself and not having any specialist knowledge would certainly appear to be a great deal less inviting.

The first and most important thing to be aware of, however, is that there are good and not so good property investment clubs and deals. A bad deal could mean you facing repossession. Having taken your money, it is unlikely

the investment club will be concerned about this and nor do they have any legal responsibility to bail you out.

The Department of Trade and Industry and the Office of Fair Trading have been investigating the property investment club business and discovered claims and promises that were so misleading that some have already been closed down. However, some clubs that offer a truly 'transparent' investing service can be an excellent starting point.

So, if you are new to investing, it's worth reading the rest of this section to get more inside information. Try two or three companies that are free or charge less than £150; see how their approach differs, what they can offer you and which you prefer.

If you are already an experienced investor, you might find the clubs useful in helping you to diversify your risk, particularly if you only have UK properties and are thinking of expanding your portfolio abroad.

> ❝ PICs can appeal to inexperienced investors, but a bad deal could result in repossession. ❞

How PICs make money

To help you to identify the good from the bad, the following methods are how investment clubs make their money. It is important to understand these points before signing up to any offers they may make you:

- **PIC courses or seminars.** Property clubs often aim to build a relationship with potential clients, sometimes by offering free 'starter' courses. Once there they can offer you opportunities that you may find difficult to refuse, but don't sign up to anything until you have been given an opportunity to check it out independently. Ask for a detailed list of what the course will cover and check what you can get free of charge from an IFA or from house price and rental surveys.

   There is a great deal of knowledge to be gained freely or at very low cost from property shows, seminars, books, magazines, newspapers articles and show and trade associations (see page 213).
- **Subscription charges.** This is money you may need to pay as a one off, annual or monthly fee to gain access to the PIC information/experts. They

 Check a PIC's financial records via Companies House (go to www.companieshouse.gov.uk) with the assistance of their company number, which should be either on their website or at the bottom of any email or headed notepaper. Speak to other investors and ask to see properties they have bought so that you can analyse whether they have made more money than general price surveys.

vary from under £100 to as much as £50,000. Compare what different clubs offer you and check their website discussion forums, which should be open and free for you to use for a period of time. Good companies may offer you a free trial – and definitely take advantage of this.
- **Selling education packs.** These might be in the form of CDs, DVDs or e-books, and typically cost around

Beware of 'get-rich-quick' schemes

Which? Magazine's article, 'Get-rich Property Schemes Exposed' tested several companies that offered 'free seminars'. After spending £6,000 on these courses, Which? concluded that the information for learning the 'secrets' of becoming a property millionaire was available elsewhere for free or at a fraction of the cost.

Property investment club checklist

It's important to realise that most PICs are not regulated. A PIC should be happy for you to check their advice independently (and even recommend you do!). In addition, do the following:

- Check the company's financial records and also get an accountant to appraise their accounts.
- Find out what you are getting from a seminar and see whether it's available free elsewhere.
- Find out how many subscribers there are and ask to meet some.
- Establish if the other investors are making money on both buying and selling.
- Ask if anyone is losing money on, say, buy to lets, and try to get this information in writing.
- Look out for money-back guarantees and ask if they have paid anyone back.
- Check costs and fees and compare them with independent services.
- Check property and rental valuations with an independent surveyor.
- Check projections and what they are based on. Ask local experts for their views.
- Make sure the sale/renting of off-plan properties are phased to prevent over supply.
- Make sure the PIC encourages you to visit the area and properties before purchase.
- Check all the information you are given with independent advisers to make sure it is accurate and fair.

£100 per pack. Watch out for companies doing quite a hard sell online or at events. Some of this information is excellent, but it is also available free online and in property papers.

Most of these packs will also be available at shows such as The Property Investor Show, where you can see the companies supplying them at seminars and visit their stand afterwards. Ideally, ask for a free sample before you commit your money and at least read a book or magazine before you go to any seminars or shows so you are in a position to see what additional information – if any – you are buying.

- **Property investment deals.** Some PICs will charge you for every property you buy, and this is not going to be cheap. Their 'discounts' of 15–20 per cent may tempt you with the promise of instant equity, but first check with independent agents if:
  - This is a real discount.
  - You can rent it out at the guideline price they have given you.
  - There is someone to sell it to when the time is right.

Charges range from nothing to 5 per cent or a PIC may charge a fixed fee (for example, £1,000 or more), or even both! Even if you get a genuine 10 per cent discount, the 4 per cent for costs and the 5 per cent fee mean that a promise of 'instant equity' will only be 1 per cent of the property's value – which is not a great deal for the work and the risks involved.

- **Selling other services.** Another way that PICs can make money from you is to sell you property related services from mortgage lenders, legal companies and sometimes surveyors, but beware – their charges may be higher than usual. Look for companies that are happy for you to use your own independent contacts. If they don't, check the deal with an independent adviser just to make sure it's right for you.

The pros and cons of PICs

Pros

- If you choose the right club, they can give you much of the information you need to assess property investments and save time identifying areas to invest in.
- Good clubs don't have a 'hard sell' approach and will be keen to be transparent in all their dealings with you, as well as keep you as a long-term client.
- Access to properties that you would be unable to buy as an individual. A PIC may buy a whole development, or part of it, and if the builder wants to sell quickly they give a discount to recoup cash. A PIC can pass on the savings to you – but check these are real.
- The most up-to-date information on tax, legal requirements and other regulations.
- Good ones should be able to advise what not to invest in, as well as potential money earners.

Cons

- Some PICs charge huge fees. Ensure you add in their costs when calculating potential gains.
- Properties for sale are only the ones they have on their books, which may not be of the investment type or in the area that you are looking for. For example, you may want to renovate a property in the Midlands, but they only have new-build/off-plan projects in the south.
- The types of investment that you can go for via some PICs are limited to buy-to-let or buy-and-hold (where you can purchase the property, leave it empty and then sell for a profit later) opportunities.
- Some deals will have such tight deadlines it is impossible to get enough time to visit the area to check them out.

Property clubs and tax

Understanding what tax you will have to pay on your property investments is as tricky and almost as difficult as finding a property investment that will deliver the returns you want.

The most important thing to be aware of with tax, is that you must have a clear idea about tax implications prior to spending your money on a property investment. If you wait until afterwards, you may end up paying a lot more tax than necessary.

Although you can seek professional advice, this can cost around £200 per hour and different experts may give different advice, further adding to the confusion. At the end of the day, it is the Her Majesty's Revenue & Customs (HMRC) that will finally decide how and what tax you will pay.

HOW PROPERTY INVESTMENTS ARE TAXED

The reason that property taxation appears to be so confusing is that it is not necessarily an individual property investment type that has a specific set of tax rules. For example, if you buy a property to rent out with the main aim being to gain an income, then income tax would usually be applied to excess rents (after costs) and capital gains tax (CGT) to the increase in the property's value when you sell.

However, this is not always the case, as sometimes all of the earnings are classed as income. This is because the

starting point from a tax perspective is to consider where you are expecting to earn your primary income from, for example:

- **Property investor,** investing in property for ongoing income.
- **Property trader,** buying property at a low price and selling relatively quickly with little/no changes to the property.
- **Property developer,** buying land/property and adding value by building or renovating for profit.

For example, you would be classed as a developer if you were to buy a property and renovate it, even if you rented it out short term. You would be a trader if you were to buy a property with a sitting tenant who then moves out within months and you sell on the property with vacant possession at a profit. If you are investing in property full time, more than one of these may apply.

Finally, if you are investing in property (whether through a syndicate, fund, land or property) with the intention of your family/friends inheriting the investments, then make sure you consult all the experts. Talk to an IFA, property tax expert and a legal expert to ensure that you mitigate the tax owed by those you leave the investments to.

Property tax tips

Here are some tips for potential ways to save on tax bills. Always speak to a tax specialist to see if any of the following tax reliefs can help reduce your bill.

- If you want your children to inherit your property but not incur a hefty tax bill, check the potential to reduce their inheritance tax (IHT). This may mean transferring ownership to them before you die or putting it in a trust.
- If you have a property investment and live in it for a certain period of time, you may be able to gain tax relief.
- As from 6 April 2008, only furnished holiday lets can take advantage of the 10 per cent 'entrepreneurs' relief on capital gains tax (CGT), otherwise the full 18 per cent applies.

You must understand how and where you intend to make your money.

SELF-ASSESSMENT VERSUS A LIMITED COMPANY

Early on you need to decide whether to declare your earnings via self-assessment or set up a company. If you do the latter, it is corporation tax that will apply. However, costs of setting up and administering a company can be high, so make sure you are fully aware of these implications before making your decision.

Questions to ask yourself prior to visiting a property tax expert are:

- How much do I (and my spouse, if relevant) earn?
- Do I want to pass my property earnings/property ownership onto my children/other family members?
- What is my objective for investing? Is it income for the short or long term, capital gains or to provide a pension?
- Am I investing alone or with others? How am I going to raise the finance?

Taxation rates for April 2008

Types of rate	Self-assessment	Limited company
Income tax from letting (profit when a company)	20%/40%	Large company corporation tax [1]: 28%; Marginal rate corporation tax [2]: 29.75% Smaller company corporation tax [3]: 21%
Capital gains tax	First £9,200 free [4]	None or little paid, it is classed as 'profit'

[1] Profits of £1.5 million
[2] Profits of £300,001–£1.5 million
[3] Profits of £0–£300,000
[4] Except for furnished holiday lets where 10% up to £1 million may apply

- What costs am I able to pay upfront? (Setting up a limited company costs around £2,000 in the first year and thereafter around £1,500 for annual audits and returns.)
- Will my investment be for letting out properties or for refurbishing and selling on? Or will it be for trading properties, buying at auction, selling via agents or buying from distressed sellers and selling on?
- Will I pay less or more more tax in the long-run following the CGT changes on 6 April 2008?

These are the types of issues that will determine the most tax-efficient way of purchase and holding (or disposing of) your property investments.

To understand the tax implications for all investments, consult property tax specialists and get the recommendations confirmed by HMRC.

Once you have established the best way to invest, then together with an adviser, work out what types of tax will apply (see the box, below) and have an idea of what tax you will need to pay.

OTHER TAX CONSIDERATIONS

Other tax considerations include:

- **Class 4 national insurance contributions (NIC)**, which are typically charged at 8 per cent of profits over £5,435, with an additional charge for profits over £40,000. These mainly apply to those who are trading and developing property.
- **Stamp duty land tax (SDLT)**, which applies mainly when you buy a

Reporting your earnings

There are three ways in which you can declare tax to HMRC:

- **Declare any income from land and property under £2,500 by filling in a P810 form.**
- **Complete the 'Income from Land and Property' and 'Capital Gains (or losses)' sections on the self-assessment form.**
- **Company tax return.**

Visit www.hmrc.gov.uk for more information and for filing online.

 Other property tax resources to go to are: www.hmrc.gov.uk, www.direct.gov.uk, www.property-tax-portal.co.uk, www.taxcafe.co.uk and www.taxationweb.co.uk. Always consult an accountant, tax adviser and HMRC for the latest rates.

Financial paperwork required

For all matters relating to tax, it is imperative to have your paperwork filed properly.

✔ **Rental income:** keep records of dates for when each property's rent starts and finishes. Use rent books to prove income (essential for weekly payments), together with receipts, invoices and bank statements.

✔ **Income earned from the sale of property:** ensure you know the date and price for the purchase of the property and the same information for any sale.

✔ **Other charges:** keep receipts for any other charges you make, such as for laundry services.

✔ **Allowable expenses:** your tax specialist will be able to advise. Make sure they are filed correctly as inaccurate information could prove costly. Some examples of allowable expenses include professional fees, such as estate agents, insurances, loan interest and, in some cases, improvements, repairs and maintenance. Keep the dates, receipts and guarantees.

✔ **Utility bills:** these exclude the phone in the property but include cost of phone calls relating to the property changes.

✔ **Council tax charges:** these may be reduced during the year. If unoccupied, you can apply not to pay any tax, if occupied by only one person you/they can obtain a 25 per cent discount.

✔ **Property advertising.**

✔ **Leasehold charges,** such as ground rent or service charges.

✔ **Capital costs:** if renting a property furnished, you may be able to claim these costs as well as costs for equipment that you may need to manage the property, for example, a computer, printer and software.

❝Keep all your paperwork in one place and don't throw out anything until you know it is no longer needed.❞

property. In some cases you may be exempt from paying SDLT, such as on residential properties bought for £120,000 (£150,000 on commercial) or less and residential properties bought for less than £150,000 in designated disadvantaged areas. There are also new rules that reduce or exempt you from paying SDLT if you purchase a 'zero carbon rated' home.

- **Value added tax (VAT).** In some cases it may be worth registering for VAT so you can claim back the VAT you pay on fees (such as estate agent fees) as well as equipment you purchase for the business. When building or developing, being VAT registered can allow you to pay lower rates of VAT, which range from 0 to 5 per cent.

TAX AND OVERSEAS INVESTMENT

If you are investing overseas, then tax becomes even more complicated as you

There will be many companies that advertise ways to reduce your tax bill. Some of these are viable, such as taking advantage of your family's different tax situations, but others may be difficult to apply legally. So make sure that you check with your own adviser that the benefits are real.

have to consider the tax in the country that you have bought in and the tax that will be applied at home.

In some cases, you pay lower taxation abroad, and then the balance of tax you would have paid had the property been in the UK. However, there are many variables at stake on this taxation, so – as ever – seek professional advice before you invest.

Top tips on tax information

- Keep your records for six years after the tax year to which they apply.
- If your property income minus expenses is less than £15,000, you can group together your income and expenses as 'totals' rather than having to break them down into individual components.
- Make sure you have filled in the self-assessment form correctly. Ideally, get a property tax specialist or accountant (with property experience) to check the information provided.
- Speak to the tax office if you have any queries.
- Don't forget to sign and date your tax return – it is one of the most common mistakes that occurs each year.

Glossary

Assignable contract: Exchange contracts to buy the property on the understanding that you can sign over your agreement to buy the property to someone else for a different price.

Assured shorthold tenancy agreement: The most common form of tenancy, at the end of which the landlord can repossess the property.

Base rate: Interest rate set by the Bank of England, which is the rate at which banks can borrow money from the Bank of England and therefore what the banks use to set their interest rates.

Bond: A vehicle that allows an investor to 'loan' his or her money to either the Government or to a company for a set interest rate return and a set period.

Break clause: A legal term inserted into a contract, such as a 12-month rental agreement that has a six-month break clause, which allows the tenant/landlord to 'break' the contract.

Bridging loan: A loan allowing you to buy a property before finalising the sale of another property.

Brownfield: Land that was previously developed for a type of use.

Building regulations: Standards of build set for new buildings, extensions and renovations.

Building warranty: Guarantee provided to cover any structural defects in a new property.

Buildings insurance: The insurance on the structure and fixtures and fittings of a property.

Buy to let: Purchasing a property to rent out to tenants.

Buying off plan: Purchasing an unbuilt new property from the plans.

Capital gains tax (CGT): Tax on profit from selling certain assets, but not including your main place of residence.

Capital growth: Increase in value of an asset, such as a property.

Class 4 national insurance contributions: National insurance contributions paid by self-employed people whose annual profits are above a certain level.

Commercial investments: These can include buying, renovating and renting a shop, office factory and/or other commercial units.

Commission: A fee based on a percentage on the selling or purchase price; can apply to an independent financial adviser as well as to an estate agent.

Commonhold: A recently introduced form of tenure offering an alternative to leasehold agreements.

Contingency: An amount of money over and above the budget to cover the cost of any unknown work.

Contract: A legal agreement such as to buy or sell a property or for a job contracted to a tradesman.

Corporation tax: Company taxation.

Covenant: A promise in a deed to do (or not do) certain things.

Deeds: The documents confirming ownership of property.

Disbursements: Costs incurred during the conveyancing process, which will be charged to the client.

Distressed seller: Someone that has to sell and is therefore willing to do so at a lower price than the market rate.

Endowment mortgage: A loan where you only pay off the interest, linked to an endowment investment policy designed to pay off the sum borrowed at the end of the term.

Equity: The difference between the price of a property sold and the loan on it.

Exchange of contracts: A binding legal agreement that confirms the intention to transfer ownership of a property between a buyer and seller.

Final sale price: The agreed price of a property that is finalised at the time of exchange.

Flipping: Buying and selling within a short period of time to take profits.

Forfeiture: A clause put in a legal contract, which means a landlord can evict a tenant even during a fixed rental term.

Freehold: Ownership of a property and the land it is situated on.

FSA: The Financial Services Authority.

FTSE: Financial Times Stock Exchange, an index based on the value of leading companies traded on the London Stock Exchange. There are two main indices, FTSE 100 and FTSE 250, which refer to the largest 100 or 250 companies listed.

Full planning permission: Approval from your local authority for you to go ahead with the property improvements as indicated in the plans you have submitted to them.

Fund manager: A specialist who chooses and manages investors' money in a particular fund or range of funds.

Gearing: The ratio of your invested money to the amount you borrowed to purchase, for example, a property.

Gilts: Short name for gilt-edged securities, which are fixed-interest or linked securities issued by the Government giving a return on your investment.

Ground rent: Payment by the leaseholder to the freeholder. Low sums are sometimes referred to as a peppercorn rent.

Hectare: A metric unit of measure equivalent to 2.471 acres.

Home condition report (HCR): The survey element of a HIP.

Home information pack (HIP): Since December 2007 this is a pack full of information about the property (mostly legal), which has to be put together before a property can be marketed in England and Wales.

House price index: Measures the change in house prices on a regional and national basis.

IFA: Independent financial adviser.

Indemnity policy: Insurance to protect a property owner in a dispute over ownership or restrictive covenants.

Inheritance tax: Tax that may be due on some gifts you make in your lifetime and on your estate when you die.

Interest-only loan/mortgage: A loan where you only pay the interest on the amount borrowed over the term of the loan.

Land certificate: Certificate confirming ownership of a property, issued by the Land Registry.

Leasehold: Ownership for a set period, most commonly applied to flats and other shared buildings.

Limited company: A business enterprise where the shareholders' liability for any losses or debts is restricted to the company as opposed to the directors.

Local searches: Information on planning and environmental matters obtained from the local authority.

Managed funds: Investment funds that invest in a broad range of shares or, more usually, in a broad range of other investment funds.

Mezzanine finance: An intermediate range of funding or investment that has a moderate degree of risk, such as some unsecured, high-yielding loans.

Mortgage: A loan for which property is the collateral.

Mortgage agreement in principle (MAP): An outline agreement to provide a loan to a specified person.

Mortgage protection policy: Life insurance taken out by the borrower so that the loan is paid off if they die or are sick (although policies do vary).

Outline planning permission: An 'approval' in principle from the local authority, given subject to gaining full planning permission.

Part-exchange: An arrangement where your home is bought by a developer (or outsourced company) to free up your monies to purchase their home.

Partnership: A company set up by two or more people who put money into the business and share the financial risks and profits.

Party wall: A wall built on a line between two adjoining properties and common to both owners.

Planning officer: A local authority employee who approves, declines and advises on changes to your property and how they might impact on nearby buildings, people and the environment.

Portfolio: A collection of financial assets owned by an individual or institutional investor.

Property funds: A pool of money that is collected from investors and invested in property (normally commercial) by an expert to achieve an investment goal.

Property investment club (PIC): Offers property deals to its members.

Property syndicates: Represent a group of individuals who pool together an agreed sum of money to invest in residential or commercial property. They are usually tied together by a legal agreement and can be managed or run by the individuals themselves.

Repayment loan/mortgage: A loan where you pay off the interest and the sum borrowed at the same time for an agreed period.

Restrictive covenant: Legal restriction on what can be done on a property or on land.

Retention: The withholding of part of a loan until any structural faults are corrected.

Reversionary bonus: The right to receive a bonus from a trust at some specified time or when some specified event occurs.

Sealed bid: Making an offer in a sealed envelope by a set date and time.

Shared ownership: Scheme where a housing association helps in the purchase of a property.

Snagging: The process of spotting the defects on new building work.

Stamp duty land tax: Tax paid when you buy property, calculated as a percentage of the price.

Subletting: When the tenant rents out a property to a third party.

Sub-prime mortgage: Loans on a property made to those with a bad credit history.

Surrender value: The amount received if a life insurance policy is terminated early.

Survey: A report on the condition of a property.

Term insurance: A life insurance policy with a time limit, usually used to cover the length of a mortgage.

Title deeds: The documents proving ownership of land.

Top-up loan/mortgage: An additional loan when the first one is not sufficient for your needs.

Unit trust: Investment in a fixed, diversified group of professionally selected stocks, bonds or other investment vehicles.

Vacant possession: When a property being sold has no one living in it.

Value added tax (VAT): Normally a 17.5 per cent tax applied to certain products and services. Some products and services are exempt from VAT and others are charged at a different rate, such as 5 per cent.

Variable rate: When the interest rate is not fixed and so can go up or down.

Void: A period when a property is untenanted and producing no rental income.

With-profits funds: Low-risk investment funds invested via an insurance policy or pension scheme. Your return is in the form of annual reversionary bonuses and also a terminal bonus.

Yield: The amount that is gained as a percentage return on the original money invested.

Useful addresses

Association of International Property Professionals
94 New Bond Street
London W1S 1SJ
Tel: 020 7409 7061
www.aipp.org.uk

Association for Project Management
150 West Wycombe Road
High Wycombe
Buckinghamshire HP12 3AE
Tel: 0845 458 1944
www.apm.org.uk

Association of Real Estate Funds (AREF)
Tel: 07720 343 792
www.aref.org.uk

Association of Residential Letting Agents (ARLA)
Arbon House
6 Tournament Court
Edgehill Drive
Warwick CV34 6LG
Tel: 01926 496800
www.arla.co.uk

Buildstore
See National Self Build & Renovation Centre

The Campaign to Protect Rural England (CPRE)
128 Southwark Street
London, SE1 0SW
Tel: 020 7981 2800
www.cpre.org.uk

Designs on Property
Tel: 0845 838 1763
www.designsonproperty.co.uk

Directgov
www.direct.gov.uk
(Produced by the Central Office of Information, Directgov provides information online from across UK government departments)

Financial Services Authority (FSA)
25 The North Colonnade
Canary Wharf
London E14 5HS
Tel: 020 7066 1000
www.fsa.gov.uk
Consumer helpline (money madeclear):
0845 606 1234
www.moneymadeclear.fsa.gov.uk

Her Majesty's Revenue & Customs (HMRC)
National advice service: 845 010 9000
www.hmrc.gov.uk

Local Authority Building Control (LABC)
137 Lupus Street
London SW1V 3HE
Tel: 020 7641 8737
www.labc.uk.com

National Approved Letting Scheme (NALS)
Tavistock House
5 Rodney Road
Cheltenham GL50 1HX
Tel: 01242 581712
www.nalscheme.co.uk

National Association of Commercial
Finance Brokers (NACFB)
3 Silverdown Office Park
Fair Oak Close
Exeter
Devon EX5 2UX
Tel: 01392 440040
www.nacfb.org

National Association of Estate Agents
(NAEA)
Arbon House
6 Tournament Court
Edgehill Drive
Warwick CV34 6LG
Tel: 01926 496800
www.naea.co.uk

National Federation of Residential
Landlords (NFRL)
8 Wellington House
Camden Street
Portslade
East Sussex BN41 1DU
Tel: 0845 456 9313
www.nfrl.co.uk/

National Landlords Association (NLA)
22–26 Albert Embankment
London SE1 7TJ
Tel: 020 7840 8900
www.landlords.org.uk/

National Self Build & Renovation Centre
Lydiard Fields
Great Western Way
Swindon SN5 8UB
Tel: 01506 409 616
www.mykindofhome.co.uk

Ombudsman for Estate Agents (OEA)
Beckett House
4 Bridge Street
Salisbury
Wiltshire SP1 2LX
Tel: 01722 333306
www.oea.co.uk

Planning Portal
www.planningportal.gov.uk

Residential Landlords Association
(RLA)
1 Roebuck Lane
Sale
Manchester M33 7SY
Tel: 0845 666 5000
www.rla.org.uk/

Royal Institution of Chartered Surveyors
(RICS)
RICS Contact Centre
Surveyor Court
Westwood Way
Coventry CV4 8JE
Tel: 0870 333 1600
www.rics.org

UK Association of Letting Agents
(UKAL)
59 Mile End Road
Colchester CO4 5BU
Tel: 01206 853741
www.ukala.org.uk

Unbiased.co.uk
Tel: 0800 085 3250
www.unbiased.co.uk
(IFA Promotions site for finding
independent financial advisers)

Website resources for property investment evaluation

Property price information
Research historical and latest property price
information.
www.hbosplc.com/economy/Housing
    Research.asp
www.hometrack.co.uk
www.landregistry.gov.uk/houseprices/
www.nationwide.co.uk/hpi/review.htm

Assessing property value

Look at properties that have sold recently and sold price data.
www.eigroup.co.uk
www.findaproperty.co.uk
www.hometrack.co.uk
www.rightmove.co.uk

Subscription websites

Helpful to research different areas to invest in and new opportunities.
www.barnsetc.co.uk
www.eigroup.co.uk
www.land4developers.co.uk
www.plotfinder.net
www.plotsearch.co.uk
www.renovatealerts.com

Property information websites

Provide information about all forms of property investment from 'how tos' to published reports and surveys.
www.assetz.co.uk
www.designsonproperty.co.uk
www.hbosplc.com/media/hbos_releases.asp
www.landlordzone.co.uk
www.propertyfrontiers.co.uk
www.propertyinvesting.net/
www.propertyinvestorsnetwork.co.uk/
www.propertysecrets.co.uk

Property tax information

www.property-tax-portal.co.uk/
www.taxationweb.co.uk/propertytax/
www.taxcafe.co.uk

Property shows and seminars

www.granddesignslive.com
www.homebuildingshow.co.uk/
www.investinpropertyshow.com
www.propertyinvestor.co.uk

Property abroad

www.assetz.co.uk
www.globalpropertyguide.com
www.knightfrank.com

Magazines

www.eigroup.co.uk
www.homebuilding.co.uk
www.property-investor-news.com
www.propertyinvestmentmagazine.com
www.self-build.co.uk

Other resources include any associations such as trade associations. See www.designsonproperty.co.uk for a full list.

Finding trades

Your first port of call should be the professional trade associations:

Builders: www.fmb.org.uk
www.buildersguild.co.uk
www.builders.org.uk
Electricians: www.eca.co.uk
www.niceic.org.uk
Heating engineers and plumbers:
www.competentpersonsscheme.co.uk
www.iphe.org.uk
www.needaplumber.org (in Scotland and Northern Ireland)
Gas fitters: www.trustcorgi.com
Architects and designers:
www.architecture.com
www.ciat.org.uk
Planning consultants:
www.rtpiconsultants.co.uk
Chartered surveyors: www.rics.org
Carpenters: www.carpenters-institute.org
Plastering and drywalling contractors:
www.fpdc.org
Garden designers: www.sgd.org.uk
Landscapers: www.landscaper.org.uk
www.landscapeinstitute.org

Index

Index

Index

which?

Which? is the leading independent consumer champion in the UK.
A not-for-profit organisation, we exist to make individuals as powerful as the
organisations they deal with in everyday life. The next few pages give you a
taster of our many products and services. For more information, log onto
www.which.co.uk or call 0800 252 100.

Which? Online

www.which.co.uk gives you access to all Which? content online and much, much more.
It's updated regularly, so you can read hundreds of product reports and Best Buy
recommendations, keep up to date with Which? campaigns, compare products, use our
financial planning tools and interactive car-buying guide. You can also access all the
reviews from *The Which? Good Food Guide*, ask an expert in our interactive forums,
register for email updates and browse our online shop – so what are you waiting for?
To subscribe, go to www.which.co.uk.

Which? Legal Service

Which? Legal Service offers immediate access to first-class legal advice at unrivalled
value. One low-cost annual subscription allows members to enjoy unlimited legal advice
by telephone on a wide variety of legal topics, including consumer law – problems with
goods and services, employment law, holiday problems, neighbour disputes, parking,
speeding and clamping fines and probate administration. To subscribe, call the
membership hotline: 0800 252 100 or go to www.whichlegalservice.co.uk.

Which? Money

Whether you want to boost your pension, make your savings work harder or simply need
to find the best credit card, *Which? Money* has the information you need. *Which? Money*
offers you honest, unbiased reviews of the best (and worst) new personal finance deals,
from bank accounts to loans, credit cards to savings accounts. Throughout the magazine
you will find saving tips and ideas to make your budget go further plus dozens of Best
Buys. To subscribe, go to www.whichmoney.magazine.co.uk.

Which? Books

Other books in this series

Buy, Sell and Move House
Kate Faulkner
ISBN: 978 1 84490 043 5
Price £10.99

Featuring the 2007 government changes to HIPs legislation. A complete, no-nonsense guide to negotiating the property maze and making your move as painless as possible. From dealing with estate agents to chasing solicitors and working out the true cost of your move, this guide tells you how to keep things on track and avoid painful sticking points.

Buying Property Abroad
Jeremy Davies
ISBN: 978 1 84490 024 4
Price £9.99

A complete guide to the legal, financial and practical aspects of buying property abroad. This book provides down-to-earth advice on how the buying process differs from the UK, and how to negotiate contracts, commission surveys, and employ lawyers and architects. Practical tips on currency deals and taxes all ensure you can buy abroad with total peace of mind.

Develop your Property
Kate Faulkner
ISBN: 978 1 84490 038 1
Price £10.99

Develop your Property is aimed at the thousands of people in the UK who are looking to make a serious and long-term investment in their property. Covering planning permission and building regulations, this guide deals with property development in a jargon-free and unbiased manner.

which?

Which? Books

Other books in this series

Renting and Letting

Kate Faulkner
ISBN: 978 1 84490 029 9
Price £10.99

A practical guide for landlords, tenants and anybody considering the buy-to-let market. Written by a practising property professional, this real-world guide covers all the legal and financial matters, including tax, record-keeping and mortgages, as well as disputes, deposits and security.

Giving and Inheriting

Jonquil Lowe
ISBN: 978 1 84490 032 9
Price £10.99

Inheritance tax (IHT) is becoming a major worry for more and more people. Rising house prices have pushed up the value of typical estates to a level where more people worry that their heirs will be faced with a large tax bill. *Giving and Inheriting* is an essential guide to estate planning and tax liability, offering up-to-the-minute advice from an acknowledged financial expert. This book will help people reduce the tax bill faced by their heirs and allow many to avoid IHT altogether.

Tax Handbook 2008/9

Tony Levene
ISBN: 978 1 84490 045 9
Price £10.99

Make sense of the complicated rules, legislation and red tape with *Tax Handbook 2008/9*. Written by *The Guardian* personal finance journalist and tax expert Tony Levene, this essential guide gives expert advice on all aspects of the UK tax system and does the legwork for you. It includes information on finding the right accountant and how to get the best from them, advice on NI contributions, tax credits for families and the self-assessment form. An indispensable guide for anyone who pays tax. This new edition, published on 14 April 2008, also contains updates from the 2008 budget and guidance on how green taxes could affect you.

Which? Books

Which? Books provide impartial, expert advice on everyday matters from finance to law, property to major life events. We also publish the country's most trusted restaurant guide, *The Which? Good Food Guide*. To find out more about Which? Books, log on to www.which.co.uk or call 01903 828557.

66 Which? tackles the issues that really matter to consumers and gives you the advice and active support you need to buy the right products. 99